Playwrights for Tomorrow

VOLUME 10

EDITED, WITH AN INTRODUCTION, BY ARTHUR H. BALLET

PLAYWRIGHTS FOR TOMORROW

A Collection of Plays, Volume 10

THE UNIVERSITY OF MINNESOTA PRESS · MINNEAPOLIS

© Copyright 1973 by the University of Minnesota

The Unknown Chinaman © copyright 1968 by Kenneth Bernard. *Fox, Hound, & Huntress* © copyright 1973 by Lance Lee. *Escape by Balloon* © copyright 1970, 1973 by W.E.R. La Farge. *Stops* © copyright 1973 by Robert Auletta. *3 Miles to Poley* © copyright 1973 by Hal Lynch.

Printed in the United States of America at
North Central Publishing Co., St. Paul

Library of Congress Catalog Card Number: 66-19124
ISBN 0-8166-0693-5

CAUTION: Professionals and amateurs are hereby warned that all plays in this volume, being fully protected under the copyright laws of the United States of America, the British Empire, the Dominion of Canada, and all other countries of the Berne and Universal Copyright Conventions, are subject to royalty arrangements. These plays are presented here for the reading public only, and all performance rights, including professional, amateur, motion picture, recitation, lecturing, public reading, and radio and television broadcasting, and the rights of translation into foreign languages are strictly reserved. Particular emphasis is laid on readings, permission for which must be secured in writing. All inquiries concerning these rights should be addressed to the author or his agent as named in the note appearing at the beginning of each play.

PUBLISHED IN THE UNITED KINGDOM AND INDIA BY OXFORD
UNIVERSITY PRESS, LONDON AND DELHI, AND IN
CANADA BY THE COPP CLARK PUBLISHING CO. LIMITED, TORONTO

Playwrights for Tomorrow

VOLUME 10

INTRODUCTION

Arthur H. Ballet

As volumes 10 and 11 of *Playwrights for Tomorrow* are published, it might be appropriate to glance back over the ten years of existence of the Office for Advanced Drama Research. At the prodding and with the financial support of the Rockefeller Foundation, and under the protective wing of the University of Minnesota, the O.A.D.R. set out in 1963 to find some way to aid theatre generally. A large order, still largely unfulfilled. But seldom are matters accomplished "generally" anyway, and soon it was apparent that if our "advanced research" was to be supportive of theatre at all, it would have to be in a specific area.

It seemed obvious that no artist worked in more lonely isolation and needed more direct contact with the theatre than the playwright. Granted the existence of contests, which promised some money and now and then a production, the fledgling playwright had few alternatives to the Big Time of Broadway or the haphazard but venturesome Splash of off-off-Broadway. Despite loud pronouncements, then as now, that theatres outside of New York were searching for new plays and writers, the evidence indicates that very few theatres really wanted to work with unknown but living playwrights. (American theatres have been sadly lacking in courage and convictions when it comes to new plays; if the Elizabethan theatre had been as shy of producing the work of new writers, it would have clung to repeats of *Gorboduc*!) The "search" for new plays was noisy and, to no one's surprise, unproductive. Theatres annually heaved a sigh of relief and went back to the classics, while the writers returned to their typewriters. Or abandoned theatre altogether.

The O.A.D.R., in its small way, has tried to open a highway (perhaps "trail" is more modest and accurate) between new, often untried writers and willing, even brave theatres. As director of the O.A.D.R., I have read literally thousands of plays, from beginning to sometimes frightening end, and I constantly search for theatres of all kinds not only really willing to work with untested material and inexperienced playwrights but also knowledgeable enough to pick that material and commit themselves to it. The O.A.D.R. has not exactly "found" great plays, but it has, I hope, found interesting writers worth encouraging.

A West Coast reviewer, I'm told, once announced that he had never seen an O.A.D.R. play he liked. I am tempted to reply that I've never read one of his columns that I liked. But more to the point, I think, is the fact that the O.A.D.R. is not an agency for *plays*, but rather a clearinghouse, a marriage broker for potential *playwrights*. Too often theatre has been the art of blaming someone else for the flop; the O.A.D.R. is committed to the playwright and not to plays or to any theories of why the arts and crafts of theatre may (or may not) be faltering.

Once a writer is "found," his work is sent off by the O.A.D.R. to be read and judged by those at theatres around the country. When a play is selected by a theatre, the O.A.D.R., with Rockefeller Foundation funds, provides some financial support to the theatre, and a per diem, travel expenses, and royalty to the playwright. Of the twenty or so plays which each year find production as a result of our efforts, perhaps five or six are published in this University of Minnesota Press series.

As with the previous volumes, numbers 10 and 11 contain a mixed bag of writing, talent, and viewpoint, but each play at least reveals a fairly distinctive voice. If most of these writers are still unknown, so much the better reason for publishing them and for encouraging theatres to do new productions of their plays.

In volume 10, the reader (and, I earnestly hope, the director) will find work by Kenneth Bernard, Lance Lee, W.E.R. La Farge, Robert Auletta, and Hal Lynch, while in volume 11 he will encounter Susan Yankowitz, David Roszkowski, Philip Bosakowski, and John O'Keefe. (I admit to a delight in publishing in one volume Yankowitz, Roszkowski, Bosakowski, and O'Keefe.)

A word or two about each of these writers may serve as an introduction to their plays.

Ken Bernard is a teacher and a critic in New York, and he has been closely associated as a playwright with John Vaccaro's Play-House of the Ridiculous. *The Magic Show of Dr. Ma-Gico* is his most recent play at the La Mama Repertory Theatre. Both a Guggenheim fellow and the recipient of a New York State Creative Artists Public Service award, Mr. Bernard writes fiction and poetry as well as plays, and his work appears in the *American Review*, in *Harper's Magazine*, and in the *Minnesota Review*. Winter House in New York has just published a collection of his plays, which consistently and often brilliantly explore the outer limits of theatre.

Lance Lee has been a lecturer in theatre arts at U.C.L.A. for the past several years. In addition to a summer at the O'Neill Playwrights Conference, he has been busy with two screenplays and a new play for the theatre, as well as working on a children's novel. His volume of poetry is "in search of a publisher."

W.E.R. La Farge has written a number of plays which have now been produced, and he has worked with several experimental theatres including the Open Stage in New York. During his residence with the Firehouse Theater in San Francisco, he enjoyed probably the longest rehearsal period in O.A.D.R. history and temporarily became a member of that commune. He writes that he is "presently working on another play." I believe him.

Two of Robert Auletta's plays, *The National Guard* and *Red Mountain High*, are being published at Yale, and the first of his plays, which the O.A.D.R. circulated unsuccessfully a few years ago to a number of theatres, *Coocooshay*, eventually was produced by Joseph Papp at the New York Public Theatre. Presently, he continues to write and to teach at the University of Illinois; his is an original, lively new voice to be reckoned with in American theatre.

Hal Lynch has been primarily an actor, but he continues to write for both the theatre and the screen. Theatre West has been his chief forum for new plays, and he has recently sold a film script for television. What he describes as an enormous movie script has grown out of what "could be said to be *3 Miles to Poley* cubed." His is a talent to be theatrical and to remember the sounds of his own past. Because he is a good actor, the memory recall is sound and often fascinating.

Susan Yankowitz has moved, with new plays, from the Open Stage in New York, to the Academy Theatre in Atlanta, to the Magic Theatre in Berkeley. She is now working on a novel at the MacDowell Colony as well as yet another new play and some shorter fiction. As a tribute to her talents, she is also the current recipient of a Rockefeller Foundation grant in playwriting to be used in residence at the Long Wharf Theatre in New Haven and of a National Endowment of the Arts fellowship in creative writing.

David Roszkowski was in Germany teaching classes when Scorpio Rising Theatre in Los Angeles elected to produce his play. International mails were terribly busy for a time in the complications of arranging the shift in locale of one of the youngest writers that O.A.D.R. has been able to get produced. He is now working in a bookstore in Hollywood and writing a novella, but *Canvas* has been produced in New York, way-off Broadway, and with some success.

Philip A. Bosakowski was formerly a teacher, but he has now decided to devote himself to writing and directing, and he hopes to start a theatre shortly in Philadelphia. He says that, confronted with various directing tasks, he found himself more and more often writing material to fit his actors and their situations and less often using the plays of others. And so he was forced into writing three plays in the last two years. Young, energetic, and talented, Mr. Bosakowski clearly has set out to create his own theatre, and he may well succeed.

John O'Keefe was collaborating with a special workshop group at the University of Iowa when the Magic Theatre in Berkeley decided to work with him on his play. As a result of that residency, Mr. O'Keefe apparently transferred himself to the West Coast permanently . . and promptly disappeared. When he reappears, I have good reason to expect he will have some new plays for the theatre.

In conclusion, let me add a personal note of gratitude and acknowledgment for patience, tolerance, and wisdom to Howard Klein and Norman Lloyd at the Rockefeller Foundation; to the Board of Directors of the O.A.D.R.: William G. Shepherd (chairman), Donald K. Smith, Willard Thompson, Michael Langham, Robert Crawford, Kenneth L. Graham, and Donald Schoenbaum; and to administrators and colleagues at the University of Minnesota. Most especially I'd like to thank Linda Wallace, the O.A.D.R.'s only hired hand, who over the years has kept the whole thing going. My thanks, through Linda, go to all of the secretaries at the university who have kept me from making greater goofs than I have.

KENNETH BERNARD

The Unknown Chinaman

for Elaine

Cast of Characters

A-M and A-F

B-M and B-F

C-M and C-F

THE UNKNOWN CHINAMAN

The play may begin with the song "Who Is the Unknown Chinaman,"
sung in darkness, or the song may be omitted.

Who Is the Unknown Chinaman

Who is the unknown Chinaman
Find him if you can
Reach out in darkness
Feel around you
Time is pressing
The hour is late

Who is the unknown Chinaman
Pigtail waving
Eyes are watching
Waiting
Waiting to speak

Who is the unknown Chinaman
His hand is inching near you
Fire or is it ice
Nails are sharp
His heart is beating
Beating inside you

Who is the unknown Chinaman
Hug him tightly

Screams are frozen
As he sits
Alone

Who is the unknown Chinaman
Find him, find him quickly
Soon he'll go away
Breath will stop
Death will find you
Find you alone

As the lights go up, three couples are lying in a comfortable middle-class living room. They are designated as couple A-M(ale) and A-F(emale), couple B-M and B-F, and couple C-M and C-F. Throughout the play, the quality of their speech, laughter, etc., is mechanical and stilted, except during the game period. Until the game period, the director may utilize any number of stylized social patterns (e.g., recognitions and greetings, cocktail poses, role playing), jammed or not. A siren sounds. Bombs explode. Screams. A baby cries. Silence. C-F sits up.

C-F
Hello? . . Anybody home? . . (*She pokes C-M, who sits up.*) Honey, are you sure they said tonight?

C-M
Of course. They said come either Sunday, Monday, Tuesday, Wednesday, Thursday, Friday, or Saturday. At any time of day or night. Hey! Anybody here?

A-F
(*sitting up*) Henry, darling!

C-M
Estelle!

A-F
Mary!

C-F
Brenda! How *are* you? (*They embrace.*)

A-F
I'm fine. How are *you*, darlings?

C-M and C-F
Fine. Just fine. Oh, we're fine. Not bad at all. Pretty good, really. Actually we're very well. How are you? Yes, how are you?

A-F

Fine.

C-M and C-F

Wonderful.

A-F

(*poking A-M with her foot*) André, look who's here.

A-M

(*standing and rubbing the sore spot*) Well — I'll be darned. Debbi! Richard! How the hell are you? (*He kisses C-F passionately.*)

C-F

I'm fine, Wendell. How are you?

A-M

(*turning suddenly to C-M and shaking his hand vigorously*) Jesus, it's good to see you, Tiger. How've you been?

C-M

Fine, Jonathan. Just perfectly fine. And you?

A-M

Fine. Wonderfully fine.

C-M

We thought for a moment we'd come at the wrong time. (*two retards to the beginning, increasing in speed and anxiety*)

A-F

(*with an intimidating tone*) And why was that?

C-M

Well . . when we knocked, no one . . (*He shrugs.*)

A-F

(*accusing*) But we *knew* you were coming. We *told* you to drop in any time.

C-M

(*defensively*) Yes, I know . . So that's why we . . called out.

A-M

And?

C-M

Well . . (*cheerfully*) *Here we are.*

C-F

(*cheerfully*) Yes. *We* knew we were coming, *too.*

A-F

(*smiling*) Well, there you are. It's really very simple.

11

C-M

Yes. (*They all laugh good-naturedly, then stand around awkwardly.*)

C-F

Is anyone else . . *coming*?

A-F

Dick and Sandra. You know, the Bonboites.

C-F

Oh, *yes*. They're lovely people.

A-F

Yes, they're very lovely people.

A-M

They've always been lovely people.

B-F

(*rising*) Did I hear my name?

A-F

Sandy!

C-F

Portia!

C-M

Yvonne!

A-M

Julia!

B-F

Hi, everybody. (*poking B-M*) Arnold, look alive.

B-M

(*sitting up*) By God, I *am* alive. Hi, gang.

OTHERS

Ugh!

A-M

(*in disgust*) Here we go again.

A-F

(*in disgust*) He's too much.

B-M

(*with a cheerful smile*) Are we late?

OTHERS

Ugh!

A-F

(*in disgust*) *That man.* (*They are awkwardly silent a few moments.*) Let's sit, everybody. (*They all sit, as if at prearranged places, and smile at each other.*) Make yourselves comfortable. (*They do, again as if it is prearranged, and smile.*) Well, there we are. Let's talk. (*They do, several times, but it is garbled and they stop abruptly each time. Silence.*)

B-F

(*to A-F*) Darling!

A-F

Jennie, dear! (*silence*)

C-M

(*to A-M*) You old son of a gun!

A-M

Damned good to see you, Craig! (*silence*)

B-M

Well. How about drinks? (*They all laugh.*) Spin the bottle? (*They laugh harder.*) I give up. (*They laugh still harder.*)

C-F

Honestly!

A-M

You're a card, Frank.

B-F

I don't know *when* I've had so much fun. You have lovely drapes. (*Silence. Suddenly they all laugh again. Silence.*)

A-M

Listen, gang, I've got this real kookie new game — (*They all laugh uproariously.*) I mean it, kids. (*a fresh burst of laughter*) Wait, I'll get it. (*He joins them in laughter, then leaves the room.*)

C-F

Honestly!

A-F

I'm telling you!

B-M

Never a dull moment with Jerry. The time just flies.

B-F

(*looking cross-eyed and hitting her head*) Bong! (*They scream laughter. A-M returns with the game, sees them still laughing, and joins in even more vigorously than they.*)

A-F

Oh, the *neighbors*. They *already* think we're just *insane*.

13

A-M

What a gas! Okay, gang, let's be serious now. (*They all laugh.*)

C-F

Honestly!

B-M

I'm going to split a gut! (*silence*)

A-F

Who invited *him*? (*laughter, gradually subsiding*)

A-M

(*reading with mock difficulty*) The Un-known Chi-na-man. (*They laugh again. He rips the package open.*) Okay, now, you quacks, let's get down to quackers. (*He laughs; they join in.*) C'mon. (*They quiet down. He hands them instruction sheets.*) This is an adult brain game. The name of the game is brain.

C-M

(*making a moronic noise*) Uhhhhh.

C-F

Honestly! (*They read their instructions.*)

A-M

All right. Have all you Chinky Chinamen read your instructions? Agnes?

C-F

Chop-chop.

A-M

Gregory?

C-M

Chop-chop.

A-M

Louisa?

B-F

Chop-chop.

A-M

Rollo?

B-M

Chop-chop.

A-M

And you, sweets? (*A-F blows him a kiss*) Good. Then we're ready.

OTHERS

(*a riot of Oriental confusion, not necessarily literal "chop-chops"*) Chop-chop, chop-chop, chop-chop, chop-chop . .

A-M

Stop! (*They stop and stare at him as if paralyzed.*) *The game begins.* (*He takes out two flashlight batteries, holds them up.*) *Two flashlight batteries with Chinese writing on them.* (*He passes them around.*)

OTHERS

(*examining and playing*) Chop-chop, chop-chop, chop-chop . .

A-M

(*holding up wires*) *Three wires, two of them two feet in length, one of them six feet in length.*

OTHERS

Chop-chop, chop-chop, chop-chop . .

A-M

(*holding up a buzzer*) *One buzzer.*

OTHERS

Chop-chop, chop-chop, chop-chop . .

A-M

(*as he connects the short wires from the batteries to the buzzer, the long one from the buzzer to the nearest chair*) Now, hear this; now, hear this. The short wires connect the batteries to the buzzer. The long wire links the buzzer to the chair. The chair is contiguous to the floor, the floor kisses the walls, the walls plunge down into the fecund earth, and the earth circles the globe. Ladies and gentlemen, we are now *plugged in.*

OTHERS

Chop-chop, chop-chop, chop-chop . .

A-M

(*to B-M*) Now, Leslie, stand here on this chair so we can see you.

B-M

(*with fake trepidation*) So long, gang.

OTHERS

Chop-chop, chop-chop, chop-chop . .

A-M

Silence! Prepare him for the asking of the question! (*They dance around him briefly, playing makeshift instruments. One puts a garland around his neck, another throws confetti at him, another puts a peach in his*

15

mouth, another sprays him with perfume. A bacchanal. Then they back away and, at a signal from A-M, begin laughing derisively at him as they point at various parts of his anatomy. At first he is not bothered, is in fact amused and inclined to laugh with them. He quickly becomes irritated, then disturbed, and holds up his hands to ward off the laughter. He tries to speak but can only grunt in protest because of the peach in his mouth.)

B-M

(spitting out the peach) Stop! Stop! Stop! *(They do. Silence. After a few moments of confrontation, A-M nods to the others. One by one they step forward and snarl insults at him.)*

B-F

Faggot!

C-M

Pimp!

C-F

Pig tit!

A-F

Vagina!

B-F

Faggot!

C-M

Mother fucker!

C-F

Pederast!

A-F

Feces head!

B-F

FAGGOT!

C-M

Butterfly gooser!

C-F

Virgin!

A-F

Dog intercourser! *(They shriek them at him together, a mad jumble of vituperation. Again he shields himself.)*

B-M

Stop! *Stop it!* STOP! *(They stop.)*

16

A-M

Of course, of course. Don't be a party poop, Winston. It's only a game. (*like a homosexual*) It's only a game, Winston.

OTHERS

(*garbled*) The question! The question! The question! The question! . . Ask him the question!

A-M

(*pacifying them*) Of course, of course, children. What else? The question. (*He snaps out a piece of paper.*) Are you ready, Antonio?

B-M

(*blinking*) Yes. I think so . . Yes. Go ahead.

A-M

Good. (*He clears his throat and reads slowly and distinctly.*) If you would receive one million dollars by pressing this buzzer that would kill an unknown Chinaman, would you do it?

B-M

(*puzzled at first, then looking at his instructions*) I don't have any instructions on that. (*He laughs a little hysterically in relief.*)

A-M

Improvise.

B-M

What?

OTHERS

(*loudly*) Improvise! (*Oriental noises*)

B-M

. . No. No, of course I wouldn't. (*The others laugh derisively.*)

A-M

Let me make your position clear. You are in new territory, I realize that. Now. You've never seen this Chinaman. No one would ever know. He would hardly be missed, if at all, there are so many of them and they're small people. He's probably a Communist and a poor neighbor. He might even be an old man, about to die tomorrow — or in a minute. Hurry. Hurry. (*He holds up the buzzer quickly. B-M makes a sudden impulsive move toward it, then withdraws.*) There would be no repercussions, no consequences. The world would go on as before, unknowing, unthinking. Just a slight pressure in one finger, any finger, and one million dollars is yours. Think of it. Think what you could do with it. (*B-M's eyes gleam. He is obviously seeing his fantasies made real.*)

17

B-M

(*snapping out of it*) No. No. It's silly. Ridiculous. No. Of course not.

A-M

(*taking money from the game*) *One million dollars?*

B-M

(*examining the money*) It's *real*. It's *real*! It's *real money*!

A-M

Of course it's real. It comes with the game. They can do this kind of thing in a socialist economy.

OTHERS

Chop-chop, chop-chop, chop-chop . .

A-M

Stop! (*silence*) Well, Edgar?

B-M

(*less sure*) I — I still wouldn't . . No. (*They laugh at him derisively.*) It's *immoral.* I have a sense of *ethics.*

A-M

Splendid. Splendid. You have *character*. (*He takes out whips and hands them around.*) You have *morality.*

B-F

Didn't I tell you he was a faggot?

OTHERS

(*screaming together*) Pig tit, pederast, feces head! . . (*A-M nods to C-M, who begins to beat B-M.*)

B-M

Ouch! Ouch!

C-F

C'mon, gang. (*They all whip him, uttering their former imprecations.*)

B-M

Stop! You're hurting me! *I don't want to play this game any more!*

A-M

Stop! Cease! Desist! (*to B-M*) I heard that. Footnote 3: No player is allowed to quit the game once begun. If he does so, he must be summarily executed. Methods may include impalement through the anus, stoning, crucifixion, crushing, disembowelment, and being put live through a meat grinder.

OTHERS

Chop-chop, chop-chop, chop-chop . . (*A-M holds up his hand. They stop.*)

A-M

Well, Gary, will you press the buzzer?

B-M

(*looking them over as he rubs himself*) No! Never! You can't make me! (*They laugh.*)

A-M

Either you're quite right or you're quite wrong. In any event, we must not hurt a man of character too much. Kill you, perhaps, but no excessive pain. (*to C-F*) Julietta, the pleasure thing, please. (*She steps up on the table and whips off her dress. Underneath she wears scant panties and bra. Her figure is luscious. She undulates slowly. A-M holds up the buzzer to B-M.*) Beautiful, no? She was Miss Tomato Paste last year, Miss French Dressing the year before. You can have her. Any way you like. You can play Queen's Lace, Darts, The Fruits of the World, Scurry-Scurry-Scat, The Man with a Hoe, The Old Clam Digger, Abracadabra, Hush Little Baby — Mama's Gone Away, Alphabet Soup, and Diddle-Diddle-Dumpling.

B-M

(*interested, but in control*) No. I won't do it.

A-M

Sure? (*B-M smiles in confidence and contempt. A-M snaps his fingers and C-F, twisting, bumping, and grinding, sings the following lyric more or less to the tune of "Save It, Pretty Mama."*)

C-F

>Kiss me, baby, kiss me,
>Good and sound.
>Kiss me, baby, kiss me
>All around.
>I got that good time feeling,
>The limit is the ceiling,
>Kiss me, baby, now.
>
>Grab me, baby, grab me,
>Here and there.
>Squeeze me like an orange

19

Everywhere.
My juice is overflowing,
I don't care where I'm going,
Squeeze me, baby, now.

So hug me, baby, hug me,
Good and tight.
Crush me, baby, crush me,
All damn night.
I got an itch all over,
Roll me in the clover,
Crush me, baby, now.

Let me have it, baby,
All the way.
Put it in the corner,
Make it stay.
I'm just about exploding
I hope that you are loading,
Baby, baby, baby,
Do it now!

(During the song, B-M is aroused and several times almost presses the buzzer. C-F stops singing but continues to move slowly, her eyes closed. Silence.)

    A-M

(softly) Just a touch!

    C-F

(passionately) George, I want you. (B-M moves his finger to the buzzer, almost touches it, hesitates, then turns away, clutching his crotch.)

    B-M

No! No! No! *(They all laugh. C-F dresses.)*

    A-M

All right, my boy. Chop-chop. Good. Virtue triumphs again. Good show. *(to B-F)* Marcia?

    B-F

(commanding) Henry, I want you to push that button. We can use the money.

    B-M

(defiantly) Why should I?

B-F

Because I'm telling you to. If you don't I'll tell everyone how you make love, how I have to comfort you when you're frightened, what you're ashamed of — (*B-M laughs scornfully.*)

A-M

Tsk, tsk, tsk. Abelard, you force me. Footnote 4: If the victim proves impervious to the inducements of ridicule, pain, greed, and lust, it is permissible to reveal the central secret of his life, that one thing which is the master cohesive factor, bringing all the disparate parts into a workable, bearable life, without which would be chaos and dissolution.

B-M

(*unbelieving*) No. You can't do that. You wouldn't.

B-F

Yes. I would and I shall.

A-M

(*taking a book out of the game*) It's in the book, anyway, Stevie.

B-M

(*to B-F*) But I trusted you. (*B-F laughs. The others join her.*) I *trusted* you.

B-F

Fool.

B-M

(*anger welling up in him*) Bitch! Helen, I beg you. It was out of love that I told you. I made myself vulnerable, defenseless, because I thought you loved me. I *gave* myself to you. I gave you *power* over me and trusted you not to destroy me. It was the truest way to show you my love. You *can't*, you *mustn't* — it would be *unholy*. It would destroy . . *everything.*

B-F

(*laughing*) Fool, fool, fool! I'll tell the world! I'll scream it from the highest rooftops! I'll blare it in the streets! My whole being will thunder it! (*a sudden, deathly silence*)

B-M

Helen.

B-F

(*deliberately*) When you were a child —

B-M

(*in a long agonizing scream full of the woe of all time since Adam*)

21

HELEN! (*He leaps down from the table, knocks B-F over, and rushes to the buzzer.*) All right! All right! I'll do it! I'll push the buzzer!

A-M

He's only a Red Chinese anyway.

OTHERS

Chop-chop, chop-chop, chop-chop . . (*B-M breaks the whips in a frenzy, stuffs the money in his shirt, and strips C-F of her clothing and humps her frantically. He then steps up to the buzzer, laughs, and presses it. There is a communal start at the presumed moment of the unknown Chinaman's death. For a few brief moments B-M looks triumphant, then, troubled, he tries to remove his finger and cannot. A look of fright, then pain, crosses his face as he realizes the truth of what is happening.*)

B-M

It's — it's — it's . . (*He crumbles slowly and dies.*)

A-M

Before you go, Montgomery, an announcement: *You* are the unknown Chinaman. (*slanting his eyes*) Velly solly. (*Each of them comes up to B-M and repeats the gesture and the words.*)

B-F

(*rising*) Gee. (*She touches B-M.*) He's really dead. That's some game. (*She begins dragging him off by the legs.*) So long, gang. Honestly!

C-M

Is that it?

A-F

(*intimidating*) Are you kidding?

C-F

You mean there's more?

A-M

(*facing the audience as the lights fade, in stage Chinese*) Ah, yes. There is more. Much more. So solly. Game go on. (*The lights continue to go down until only his face is visible.*) So velly solly. There is more. Much, much more. Humble Chinaman velly solly. But there is more. Much more. Velly solly. (*Complete darkness. Softly, as if urging audience.*) Chop-chop? You speakee chop-chop? Chop-chop. Chop-chop. Chop-chop . . (*in a whisper*) Chop-chop. (*"Velly solly" chant fades into muted sounds of siren, bombs, screams, and a baby crying. Silence. Perhaps a light pattern on the tableau.*)

THE END

The Unknown Chinaman by Kenneth Bernard was presented on July 8–25, 1971, at the Magic Theatre, Omaha, Nebraska. It was directed by Jo Ann Schmidman. The performers were Frank Goodmann, Susan Juvelier, Jon Kaiser, Bill La Barge, Charlie Pollock, and Connie Spirit. For the Omaha production the author wrote additional songs and lyrics. These were also used in a subsequent production at Brecht West Theater, New Brunswick, New Jersey.

LANCE LEE

Fox, Hound, & Huntress
A COMITRAGEDY

Cast of Characters

FOX
HOUND
HUNTRESS

Time: coming . .

FOX, HOUND, & HUNTRESS

Before rise: There is no curtain. Down right there is a crate, used as a seat and stump; adjacent, a trashcan. Down left there is part of a broken wall. Up center we see a perhaps seven-by-ten-foot flat painted with a slum alley scene, on which are hung the separate pieces of the manikins — both male — the Fox will use later in his creation of Hound and Huntress. The lights fade out. There is the sound of a foxhunt: horses, baying dogs, wild cries, panting we might guess to be Fox's, gunshots, curses, mingled with brief flashes of traffic sounds and an accident in which something living is hit, all mixed with snatches from songs — hunting, popular — and from well-known classics. This crescendos and fades as the lights rise. The lighting is bright, arid, and constant.

At rise: Fox, a bottle of Chianti in one hand, enters singing along with the end of the soundtrack. Fox is an actor dressed, very loosely speaking, like a red fox (trousers, not tights, etc.), with a fox mask (quite real and frightening) so worn that the snout projects over his forehead without obscuring his face. When he notices the audience, he drops his head (displaying the mask) briefly, surveying the situation. Almost immediately he continues.

FOX
Tally ho! Tally ho! Woof! Woof! (*brief pause as he digests the audience*)
　　　　A hunting we will go! Woof ho!
　　　　A huntering we were gone! Arf! Argh!

27

Hunting long ago!
Tantivy tantivy tantivy!
A hunting we would go!
Ahh, those were the days!
(*declaiming to audience*)
  "Before the pack for many a mile
  A fox had sped in gallant style;
  But gasping with fatigue at last,
  The clamorous hounds approached him fast —"
(*imitatively*) Woof ho! Ow-oo! Yapyapyap! Arf! Argh! (*slight pause*) Oh
for a hound. For a hunter. For death. (*declaiming*)
  "Though painful now the toilsome race,
  With dirtied tail and stealthy pace
  Still onward for his life he flies —"
(*drinking*) Flies, flies, flies! (*He abruptly breaks off: the memories he is
struggling against start to come through.*)
  He nears the alley — 'fore him lies
  A tangled mass of — glass — and wire —
  In vain he 'neath the — barbs aspires . .
(*slight pause; declaiming*)
  "So springing, heedless of his skin,
  With desperate bound he leaps within!"
(*He leaps into the trashcan. Simulated cries.*) Ow! Ooo! Ouch! Ohh! . .
What a great tradition the hunt was! (*slight pause*) But where are the
hounds of yesteryear? Awoo! Oh where are the foxhounds that hunting
used to go, to go, hunting used to go, woof! Arf! Awoo . . (*slight
pause*) Not even Grandmother remembered the last hunt. (*slight pause*)
I could as well ask, where are the foxes? (*He glances at the trashcan he
is still in. A slight pause: melancholy descends.*) The city is my forest.
The city — is — (*He remembers.*) The city is my laboratory! I mustn't
think of this. I'm — I'm — (*He tries to escape into triviality again, climbing out of the trashcan.*) I'm the last fox left in the ecosystem on this
biosphere. I like Chianti. (*He takes a swig.*) Bad Italian food. Sulphur in
the air because it hides my scent. Old derelict trucks. With derelicts in
them. Nags, bags, bores, whores. Empty pillboxes without labels. I even
like monumental cataracts of traffic. They eliminate cats and dogs. Cats,
because they eat what I eat. Dogs — what's a dog but a four-legged man
with a simple attitude to life and unhygienic practices? Awoo . . (*He
shrugs, takes a swig.*) Trash! in particular. Mountains, suns, rivers of

trash! Full moons and white stars of trash! Over warrens of trash, trash, trash! Cool hiding places. A fetid smell. A sense of foxhome. (*Pause. He has trapped himself.*) In the wastes . . (*pause*) In the alley, the — babies — (*pause*) Where is my sister! Where are my children! Mustn't remember this . . Where are my murderers! Mustn't, Shouldn't! Can't! Hound! Hunter! (*Pause: he struggles for control. He puts the Hound and Hunter together in the hunt demonstration.*) It's a hell of a thing to be the last fox. To be the hunted animal par excellence: and suddenly — no one wants you anymore. They've forgotten. (*pause*) I mean, if no one comes after you, you're worthless. (*Pause: he shakes his head.*) If there's no hound around the corner — (*mixes action with description*) snuffle, snuffle — no hunter behind the door — snuffle — no booted foot stepping into the alley — into the woods! (*He freely mimes a hunt with the manikins, breaking it with abrupt asides.*) Woof! Oh, no! Woof woof yapyapyap! Hounds! Ow-oo! Thank God! (*aside*) No teeth in the dark hole — no cocked guns — (*hunt*) Bangitty bangbang! Trapped! I'm trapped! (*He hides his head in the can. Aside*) No smoke brands, no flashing eyes! (*hunt*) They're everywhere! This is just the thing! How horrible! (*aside*) No blood — no pelt — no cry of triumph — I mean, who are you? (*hunt*) Down the dark hole, lost in the dark maze — drowned in — formaldehyde . . (*Pause: he regroups into traditional hunt imagery.*) Down, drowned — fangs! in the dark hole — (*slight pause*) Dead beyond all hope — (*slight pause: yelling to his "hunters"*) I won't come out! (*aside*) Better dead than — (*hunt*) I won't come out! (*aside*) Than as — I am — (*hunt*) I WON'T BE SMOKED OUT! (*aside*) Completely individual. (*hunt*) Sticks and stones may break my bones — (*aside*) Utterly unique! (*hunt*) But smoke will never hurt me! (*He laughs wildly, and is seized by an agony of coughing. The sounds of the foxhunt reprise, sharp: he screams.*) Teeeeeeeeerrrrrrriiiiiiibbbblllleeee! (*The sounds augment: he hastily pulls himself together and stares: he drops his head displaying the mask and "looks" back and forth in the fast blackout. The foxhunt sounds fade. We become aware of a lingering snuffling and growling that grows on its own. In the darkness, Fox's voice rings out in fear.*) What the hell! (*The growling continues. Fear and delight.*) What the — hell . . (*The growling becomes savage.*) Ouch! Quit it! Hell and damnation on your wirehaired ass! Ooo! Ow! Foxgod! A hound! A houououounnnddd! Thank you, God! HELP!

(*The lights rise. The manikins are gone. Fox is backed against the manikin wall by Hound. Hound's face is clear, the mask pushed up over his fore-*

head, like Fox's. Trousers, not tights, like Fox. Hound is lunging at Fox, who barely manages to fend him off.) I've heard of being up against the wall, but this isn't real! Hey! Ooo! (*Hound throws an occasional knowing glance at the audience. Enter, languidly, with an M-16, a stunning, sex-goddess, white-jumpsuited, with-it Huntress. Hound groans. Fox gasps. He lowers the mask and surveys the scene before he reacts. Slight pause.*) You've got to be kidding . . What a way to go . . Awoo-oo-ooo! Hey! Back off, will ya? Come on, baby, here I am! Oh thanks, Foxtrinity, I'm going to get it at last! OUCH! Madam, I can't wait for your performance! OOO! Away! Beast! In the foxful words of Sir Thomas More, my spirit is blithe to go! Get off my BACK! In the foxless words of Nathan Hale I regret I have only one life to offer for my extinction! Oww! Ohh! Help! Not this way! Shoot me up! NOOOOOWW! (*Hound has got Fox by the throat and is gleefully strangling him. Huntress snaps her fingers and stamps her titillating foot. Hound instantly leaps away and cowers. Fox proudly draws himself up.*) There is a far far better thing we could do to fulfill this extremity. (*Fox is in a self-conscious fig-leaf stand. He smiles. She raises her gun. He freezes. She slowly gyrates her hips.*) Ohhh . .

HOUND

Ahhh . . (*Her tongue emerges from her cheek to one side of her lips.*)

FOX

Oooo . .

HOUND

Owww . . (*She tosses her head and breathes deeply, emphasizing her breasts. Fox falls to his knees.*)

FOX

Please.

HUNTRESS

Reeeaaadddyyyyyy?

FOX

Aaaaaaaaaammmmmmmm Iiiiiii eeeeeeever!

HUNTRESS

(*with a sensuous, explosive movement*) Baaaaaaaaaaaaaaaaaaaannnnggggg! (*The gun clicks. A banner is thrown over the manikin wall: Death Is Such a Cliché. Fox does not see it. He opens his eyes to the laughter of Hound and Huntress.*)

FOX

Baaannngg . . Is that all? Click? (*pause*) Nothing else? (*pause: disappointedly outraged*) At least my father was hit by a Food Giant truck!

That's not much, but it had size! My mother got run over by an AAA repair truck! Wasn't that a stupid way for a woman to go? But she went!
They always do go! And my grandmother and grandfather got it the
next best way, mistaken for stray dogs and shot! At least shot! Even as
dogs! You never go the way you want to! But bbbbbbbbbbbaaaaaaaaaa-
nnnnnnnnnnggggggggggg! What's this baaaaaannnnggg? Baaaaaaaaaa!
Nnnnnnnnnnn! Ggggggggggg! (*desperate*) I was ready and waiting: one!
Smoke? No thanks . . Two! Blindfold? Wrong shape head, you'd have
to tie it under my chin. Oh, quite right . . Three! BANG! ARGH! (*He
falls backward: both the others are in hysterics. On his back he at last
sees the banner.*) Death — is — such — a —cliché — (*pause*) Death is
such a cliché. (*Their laughter has died.*)

ALL

Death is such a cliché. (*The lights dim, but do not black out. They freeze.
Long pause. The lights rise to full. Hound, stylized and having fun putting Fox on, moves in on him again. The soundtrack, faintly heard,
dies.*)

HOUND

Snuffle. Grrrr.

FOX

Hey! Now hold off! We're not going through this again!

HOUND

Snuuuuufffle! Grr!

HUNTRESS

(*arresting Hound's movement*) Houououounnnd . .

HOUND

Hm?

HUNTRESS

Houououounnnd . .

HOUND

Grrg! What do you want?

HUNTRESS

It's tiiiime . .

HOUND

(*scratching himself, eyeing Fox, and deciding to go for him for real*) I
dunno what you want.

HUNTRESS

Tiiiime toooo begiiii — iin.

HOUND

Begin what! I want him now! GRR!

FOX

oww!

HUNTRESS

HEEL! (*Hound pulls back a little.*) Come here, Hound.

HOUND

I don't want to.

HUNTRESS

HOUND! Youou know . . (*Hound half-willingly comes to her. At a gesture, he curls at her feet. He begins "cleaning" himself as she talks. Fox cautiously draws nearer.*) You know how it is, darling Hound . .

FOX

(*muted*) Darling?

HUNTRESS

(*watching Hound lick himself*) You know that won't do any good. (*He embraces her feet.*) Or that! You have to lie before the fire, darling, the flames must collect in your — veins — you know how it is . .

FOX

What is . .

HUNTRESS

C'mon, sweetie pie. Mommy's baby booby hounddy boy . .

FOX

That's a hound's life? (*Huntress has leaned over and begun tickling Hound's midriff. She soon starts masturbating him.*)

HOUND

Ermph.

HUNTRESS

You want to please me, don't you?

HOUND

(*fighting his laughter and pleasure*) Ermph. Umph! No. Ohh. Hoo!

HUNTRESS

Ohh youou doo . .

HOUND

Oh, no . . Ha! Ho! No!

HUNTRESS

(*rougher*) Own up! (*One leg, doglike, begins jerking.*)

HOUND

Oh ho what haha do you haha hoo! want?

HUNTRESS

Own up!

HOUND

Oh ha no oh ha! Yes! No!

HUNTRESS

You want to please yourself, don't you?

FOX

What a — hunter . .

HOUND

Yes! No! More! No more!

FOX

Oh ho what haha are they haha up haha to? (*Hound's sounds become sensuous as the rubbing continues. Huntress drags him a little to the wall while he is absorbed in himself. She attaches a chain to collar and wall. Then she steps back.*)

HUNTRESS

Ooooooo, Hououououound! Ohh! You looook reeaaddyyy!

HOUND

Unhunhuhunhunhuhhunh ahahahahaahaah Iiiiiiii'm gettiiiiinnnnngggg haaaarrrrd!

FOX

Seeing is believing!

HUNTRESS

Hound, I'm soo ready!

HOUND

Oh ha ha ho ah ha! (*He is oblivious to the chain and paws at the ground.*)

HUNTRESS

There's my horse! C'mon! Let's go for a ride! (*He neighs.*) There's my bully boy! (*He snorts.*) Lower your — horn! (*He drops his head and wags his rear.*) Here's the cape — (*She sways in front of him.*) Come gore me! (*Fox is moving nervously back and forth. Hound snorts, neighs, backs up, and throws himself forward. The chain jerks him backward. Defiantly*) Come gore me, you limp dog you! (*Hound picks himself up and hurtles forward again, with the same result. Fox stares unbelieving.*)

FOX

No, Hound . . Stop him, Huntress! (*Huntress finds Hound very amusing. He throws himself forward again, and once again. Fox cries out each time as if the pain were his.*)

HOUND

It's not fair! I didn't even notice! I'll get you! I'll — get — you! I'll ooo arth! AH! (*He attacks the chain desperately. Fox begins to laugh with Huntress. They move together and share the torment. Transported with rage, Hound flings himself forward one last frenzied time, crying sharply in his pain as the others laugh. Blackout. Pause. The lights rise on Fox trying to open a new bottle of Chianti. Huntress stares vaguely at the audience or lays it on for Fox.*)

FOX

Om. Um. Am. Damn!

HUNTRESS

Why don't you take the wrapping off?

FOX

The wrapping. (*He stares at her.*)

HUNTRESS

The wrrrrap! Ping!

FOX

Ohh . . (*He peels it off after a slight pause, then struggles with the cork.*) Om. Um. Am. Damn! . . Like some?

HUNTRESS

Suurree . .

FOX

It's good even bad! Haha . . (*He offers the bottle to her after he takes a swig. She stares at it with distaste.*) What's wrong?

HOUND

(*despondency personified*) She's a lady.

FOX

Mind your own business.

HOUND

You don't know much about lady — animals — do you, Fox? They need a glass, and then they need someone to pour it for them, and then they need a toast, like, haha, blood in your eye . .

FOX

What kind of toast is that?

HOUND

Then they drink with their little pinky sticking out. Sort of a "come on."

HUNTRESS

Smart dawgy. (*She crooks her finger. Hound's despondency momentarily vanishes in his desire.*)

34

HOUND

Let me go then!

FOX

You'll keep him chained?

HOUND

I've never been chained before!

FOX

She chained you this time at least!

HUNTRESS

(*to Hound*) You chained yourself!

FOX

What are you saying?

HOUND

You chained me!

HUNTRESS

(*to Hound*) You're an inveterate liar. (*to Fox*) It's sad.

FOX	HOUND
You chained him.	You chained me!
I saw you.	He says so!
I thought he was going	I thought I was going
to kill himself!	to kill myself!

HUNTRESS

HahahahahaHAHAHAHAHAHA . . (*pause*)

HOUND

I don't care how it happened. Help me . .

FOX

Chain him —

HUNTRESS

He chained himself! Let him undo it!

FOX

You're the liar.

HOUND

I WANT TO BE FREE!

HUNTRESS

HE'S MY LAST FOX! (*Pause. They stare at her. The force was unexpected. She seems anything but sensuous for a moment.*)

FOX

There are a, ah, few things I don't — follow —

35

HUNTRESS

This is how we begin.

FOX

This isn't how grandmother described the hunt!

HUNTRESS

This is how we are! (*Slight pause. Fox stares, mask down, bewildered.*)
Is the chain heavy?

HOUND

Very —

HUNTRESS

(*like ice*) Frustration is good for you.

HOUND

No —

HUNTRESS

You like pain.

HOUND

I'd like to come into the warmth —

HUNTRESS

You need stimulation. (*Hound is stung by the contempt and Fox's
pleased expression.*)

HOUND

I'll show you my stuff! Just let me go!

FOX

He'll eat me if you don't keep him chained!

HUNTRESS

(*simultaneously, to Hound*) Shut up!

HOUND

Humh?

HUNTRESS

Lie down!

FOX

Lay it on!

HOUND

I'll get you both for this!

HUNTRESS

Kiss your chains!

HOUND

You're inhuman!

FOX, HOUND, & HUNTRESS

HUNTRESS
Oh be quiet, dog!

HOUND
I will not.

HUNTRESS
Heel, Hound. Obey!

HOUND
(*attacking his chains and her, as far he is able*) I'm meant to hunt! To woof woof woof! Yapyap yapyap! Owoo! Ow-oo-oo!

FOX
(*he and Hound build to pandemonium*) Pantpantpant! Arfpantarfpant! Arfarfarfarf! Yapyapyapyap! Awoo! Awoo-oo-oo!

HUNTRESS
I'VE HAD ENOUGH!

HOUND
NOT LIE BY THE FIRE LIKE A STUFFED TROPHY!

HUNTRESS
(*miming a whip*) QUIET!

HOUND
Ooo!

HUNTRESS
Down!

HOUND
Oww!

HUNTRESS
You uncouth beast!

HOUND
Aaa!

HUNTRESS
You slobbering slophound!

HOUND
Uuhhuh!

HUNTRESS
You Blood-Stained Stinking Prick-Hanging —

HOUND
EEK!

HUNTRESS
SON OF A BITCH!

HOUND

AA! OO! OW! AH! (*He twists in agony as the "beating" climaxes. Huntress stands sobbing above him. Fox stumbles in fear across the stage, gasping.*)

FOX

No, Hound — go away — Huntress —

HOUND

Please don't stop . . I do crave attention . . I do need your caresses . . Pet me some more . . Any mark of affection or attention is joy to my oo! (*She kicks him. Crying*) Go on! Go On! (*Pause. They stare at him.*)

HUNTRESS

If you're not quiet I'll muzzle you.

HOUND

You wouldn't.

HUNTRESS

Wouldn't I? (*She goes over to the manikin wall, removes the muzzle dangling there, swings it around her pinky. Pause.*)

HOUND

What's happened between us?

HUNTRESS

Nothing. (*pause*) We've had lots of things before. Rabbit types. Sheep types. A horse once. Fish types. Guinea pigs! Other dogs.

HOUND

Noo.

HUNTRESS

Other hounds.

FOX

Jesus Foxchrist. (*pause*)

HUNTRESS

But I really can't remember a fox before. (*Pause. She stares at Fox. Hound is muttering.*) Not the last fooox. Nooooot Beeefooooorrrrrr. (*pause*) So quiet, or . . (*She waves the muzzle.*) Chained, beaten, muzzled, forgotten. (*Pause. She sighs.*) I'd like some wine now. (*pause*)

FOX

(*fascinated and cautious*) There're no glasses.

HUNTRESS

Foxes are supposed to be cunting.

FOX

(*nervous laughter*) Cunning, ah . . Some.

HUNTRESS
(*touching him*) Cunting . .

FOX
Some . . (*mesmerized by her closeness*) Ah . .

HOUND
Ow-ooo!

HUNTRESS
(*ignoring him: to Fox, moving against him*) C'mon . . Uuuussseee your imagination . .

FOX
Maybe I could — maybe — oh my! pour it ah, in haha a little at a time hahaha —

HUNTRESS
Hahaha —

FOX
In your mouth! if — you still — want — it —

HUNTRESS
Ooo what a gooood idea . .

FOX
Imagine: you — me — haha . . (*She laughs and tilts her head back, opening her mouth. Fox stares nervously, then carefully tilts the bottle. Her hands gesture for more: he continues pouring. The wine runs out of her mouth. Hound becomes frenzied with a mix of anger, desperation, and sexual excitement.*)

HOUND
Ohh, you bitch you. If only you were. A bitch! I'd know what to do. (*Fox has turned on this, still pouring: the red wine runs down her white jumpsuit.*) Look what you're doing! Oaf! (*Fox steps back in shock. He licks her fingers.*) Ow-oo!

FOX
What a fool I am! That looks like — I need a rag — ah — a rag — no glasses, no rags. Fox! a cunning oaf —

HOUND
Cunting!

HUNTRESS
THAT WAS VERY NICE! (*Pause. Hound cringes. Another banner, Tally Ho, is thrown over the manikin wall, again unnoticed by Fox.*)

FOX
Nice?

HUNTRESS

(*closing*) Why are you trembling, Fox?

FOX

Am I really? (*He backs off.*)

HUNTRESS

You're a virrginal type fooox . .

HOUND

I may be a dog, but she's too much!

HUNTRESS	HOUND	FOX
I don't like noisy hounds.		
I don't like your tongue.	You did!	Easy come easy go!
Your hair.	It's so velvet!	Long red sticky-licky thing.
Your revolting sad eyes.	You teased my hair!	Mine is natural.
Or your tail!	They're so compassionate.	Mine are bright and beady.
	You liked to see it move!	Oh he's vulgar!

HUNTRESS

(*wholly attentive to Fox, still oblivious to the banner*) How could I ever touch him?

HOUND

How you used too . .

HUNTRESS

Foxy dearie, booby dooby-pie, we'll have such intimacies.

FOX

Ummm . . Maybe . .

HUNTRESS

Hahahaha . .

HOUND

We used to have such intimacies . .

FOX

Give it up, dawgy . .

HUNTRESS

Hahahaha . .

HOUND

Your balls will be mine, buddy!

HUNTRESS

You need them!

HOUND

I never dreamt in any dog-eared moment you'd be mucking about with a fox, letting him pour his wine all over you, licking your fingers!

FOX

Heeyy . . He's jealous!

HUNTRESS

So he is! Silly dog!

HOUND

Heaving your breasts! (*As he says the words, she does so, looking deeply at Fox.*) Just like that!

FOX

What breasts!

HUNTRESS

Silly boy!

HOUND

Weakening at the knees! (*She stretches out her arms to Fox as she slowly sinks down.*) Just like that!

HUNTRESS

Hahahaha . .

HOUND

You're supposed to be hunting him!

HUNTRESS

Here Fox, here you bright-eyed bushy-tailed unsuspecting —

HOUND

You loose-limbed —

HUNTRESS

Little hairy thing you-ou-ooo!

HOUND

Sodomistically —

FOX

Inclined —

HOUND

Whore!

HUNTRESS

Here Foxy . . Come . . Come . .

FOX

Why not? Come . . Coming . .

HOUND

(*raging at the chain as Fox sinks onto her*) FOX! WATCH OUT!

FOX

Hunh?

HOUND

She's supposed to kill you! (*Fox half lifts himself up.*)

HUNTRESS

Ignore him, sweetie . .

HOUND

Oh, no — not in front of me! FOX! She's supposed to kill — kill! KILL! OH how I'D like to KILL YOU!

FOX

(*breaking away*) That's right . .

HOUND

To feed you.

HUNTRESS

Hound —

HOUND

To groom you . .

FOX

What's he trying to say?

HOUND

To make a lapdog out of you —

HUNTRESS

Hound! . . Ignore him, sweetie. He's an inveterate liar —

HOUND

To domesticate you!

HUNTRESS

Hound down!

HOUND

So you'll curl up before the fire, fur on the cream-hued trembling landscape, the moving mountains, ohh the sinking valleys, the tumultuous odor of earth under the reynard-colored beating sun, the animal, sinking under his own desire, bound! by his desire!

HUNTRESS

Dog heel!

FOX, HOUND, & HUNTRESS

HOUND

Chained! Beaten! Muzzled! Forgotten . .

HUNTRESS

Forgotten! (*She has gotten up and moved threateningly toward Hound who continues under a growing fear.*)

FOX

Go on, Hound!

HOUND

She's going to kill you, Fox, remember?

HUNTRESS

You've been warned!

HOUND

To kill you — JUST LIKE ME!

HUNTRESS

You know what's coming, dog!

HOUND

(*uninterrupted*) Like I was before — I was before — before you —

HUNTRESS

HEEL HOUND!

FOX

What?!

HUNTRESS

YOU'RE RUINING THE CHASE!

HOUND

HOW DO YOU KNOW THAT I WASN'T A FOX ONCE?

HUNTRESS	**HOUND**	**FOX**
AI!	OH!	OO!

(*Huntress attacks Hound in a frenzy. Fox finally pulls her off the cringing, weeping beast.*)

FOX

Here! Calm down! He's only a — doggone, you two complicate things! Madam — rest easy — I say! See, he's quiet! Yes, there, there . . Hey! What are you doing? (*She has begun to turn her emotions into amorous designs on him, going from one violence to another.*) The mood's a little dented! What in hell did he mean by all that?

HUNTRESS

Never mind, foxy-woxy dearie, oh I love red hair, red eyes —

FOX

Leave me alone! (*He dumps her on the stump.*)

43

HOUND

She'll get you, Fox . .

FOX

What did you mean by saying —

HOUND

You poor hung-up bastard . .

FOX

By saying you were a —

HOUND

She doesn't like to be refused!

FOX

FOX! (*slight pause*)

HUNTRESS

What are you up to, Hound?

HOUND

He's my last fox too! (*pause*)

FOX

I wish I was a man.

HOUND

(*mocking*) He wishes he was a man!

HUNTRESS

Why's that, Foxy?

FOX

I wouldn't need you, Hound —

HOUND

(*to Huntress*) Huntress —

HUNTRESS

(*to Fox*) FOX! (*Fox lowers his mask. Slight pause. He looks back up.*)
I'm master here. (*Pause. Hound cowers.*)

FOX

There're a few things I have some say about!

HUNTRESS

Come whisper all the sweet nothings you like in my ear, dearie . .

FOX

You stay away from me . .

HOUND

What the hell. Don't let my being here inhibit you, Fox. Can't you do
"it"?

FOX
Oh, c'mon!
HUNTRESS
What are you up to, Hound?
HOUND
What if he can't? All show? He's the end of the line!
HUNTRESS
The end of the line . .
FOX
Hey, what are you implying?
HUNTRESS
Can't you "do" it?
FOX
Oh c'mon now! That's a low blow haha Hound haha Huntress!
HOUND
Foxes were always inadequate —
HUNTRESS
Frightened —
HOUND
Hung-up —
FOX
I've had lots.
HOUND
Virrrginaaal —
HUNTRESS
You're the last fox. We know.
HOUND
He's never had anyone. He doesn't know how. Or by now he can't!
FOX
That's an ignorant stab in the dark!
HOUND
Talk, talk!
HUNTRESS
Frightened —
HOUND
Hung-up —
HUNTRESS
Who, Fox, who's been before?

FOX

Lotsa! Lotsa — lotsa — (*They build the "Talk, talk!" "Frightened —"
"Hung-up-" "Who, Fox, who's been before?" to a crescendo as Fox
interjects and begins saying more than intended under the pressure.*)
It's not talk. Hey, how'd you get on this? There have been lots. What is
this, a trial? I won't say. I can too! There were — not all that many, I
am the last! In the alley! Dammit the alley! And there were — No Hound!
No Huntress! stop — NO HOUND NO HUNTRESS STOP all my children —
are dead! I'm the end of the line THE LINE THE LINE THE LINE THE LINE
the line the line . . (*He fades into sobs. Pause.*) I am the last fox . .
I want to be alone . . (*pause*)

HOUND

She's going to get you. (*pause*)

HUNTRESS

Do it now, Fox.

FOX

How could I — remembering —

HOUND

Free me! It was all talk!

HUNTRESS

Do it now, Fox! (*She is markedly stalking him.*)

FOX

What the hell . . You're my hunter —

HUNTRESS

Huntress . .

HOUND

Hunter, male; huntress, female . . (*slight pause*)

FOX

I'm willing to let you kill me — if you can catch me —

HOUND

Oh she'll get you!

FOX

That's a fox's primary principle! But no more!

HOUND

You're a stupid fox.

FOX

Don't say that!

HUNTRESS

I like this hunt! (*Slight pause. She turns him to see the banner, and runs her hands down his sides.*)

FOX

Tally ho. (*pause*) Incredible. (*slight pause*) The times have really passed me by.

HOUND

Ow-oo!

FOX

Awoo!

HUNTRESS

Tally ho! (*pause*) Come and get it, Foxy.

FOX

(*twists away, but is maneuvered up against the wall; eyes bulging*) Fox-shit.

HUNTRESS

Up against the wall, Fox! (*The hound begins jerking at his chains methodically and forcefully.*)

FOX

Wha — whaa — what about him —

HUNTRESS

I know the strength of my own chains —

FOX

Yours? His? Whose?

HUNTRESS

I'm going to lay one on you tooooo . .

FOX

That was only a metaphor . . (*She has undone his shirt.*)

HUNTRESS

Ohh, noo . . (*Hound's animal sounds build in desperation as he struggles to break free. He pauses intermittently only to stare at them, then with more vigor returns to the attack.*)

FOX

You're not kidding, are you . .

HUNTRESS

Ohh, noo . .

FOX

I never thought being skinned could be so painless . .

HUNTRESS

You can skin me too . . See . . (*She pulls the zipper down her jump-suit.*)

HOUND

Arrrh. Errr! Arareor!

FOX

Great — foxtits . .

HUNTRESS

I like this hunt veery much. (*He is stripped to the waist.*) Nice . . (*She runs her hands over him, then, grabbing his, places them on her. He lets them run down her.*)

FOX

Ooo . . What . . Flesh . .

HUNTRESS

Touch . .

FOX

Ohhh . . (*His trousers drop as she rubs his genitals; he squirms. Note: her back is to the audience; she stands in front of Fox.*)

HUNTRESS

I like taming you . .

FOX

Ohhh . . Ahhh . . Ummm . .

HUNTRESS

Exciting . . Chasing . . Catching . . (*They're sagging and clinching as Hound, with a huge exertion, tears free.*)

HOUND

AHH! FREE! YOU BEAUTIFUL CHAIN YOU! (*He lashes around the stage with it. The soundtrack comes on louder, mixed with hoarse panting and a woman's cries. Fox and Huntress spring apart. Hound, with a blow and length of chain, savagely knocks Fox down and out. Hound as force-fully attacks the — happy — Huntress.*)

HUNTRESS

Oh, Hound, you dog you! (*Blackout. The sounds of panting and crying with the hunt build very fast and fade as quickly. The lights rise abruptly on Fox. He is standing with the gun.*)

FOX

Get up, Hound. Come on, Hound! Off! Up! (*Hound staggers off Hunt-ress, laughing at the sight of Fox. Huntress lolls where she is, humming snatches of popular songs.*)

HOUND

Oh ho haha . . You'll hurt yourself. (*He lashes with the chain. Fox leaps back.*)

FOX

I'll shoot!

HOUND

You'll break thousands of years of fox-hunting history!

FOX

You just broke thousands of hounding.

HOUND

Every woman has her hound. You're an urbane fox. You've seen them. Usually they look like poodles. Sometimes they walk on their rear legs. It's all the same. The leash. (*He lashes out.*) The obedience. The grooming. And they all hang out. You know how it is. (*lashing*) I'm going to make you lick mine. (*lashing*) Stupid Fox.

FOX

Don't say that!

HOUND

(*maneuvering him against the broken wall, lashing occasionally*) You've never used a gun, Fox. (*slight pause*) Dumbass.

FOX

I told you!

HOUND

Your safety is on! (*Fox looks down momentarily. Hound leaps at him and he falls back over the wall and just manages to roll away from Hound's chain.*) Oh! Ho! Ha! Ha! Faced down by a dog and a chain!

FOX

I'll get you!

HOUND

Willing to be seduced by his hunter —

FOX

Huntress! Hunter, male; huntress, female!

HOUND

Willing to be turned into a living ornament! Unload! (*He throws his arms wide and waits for Fox to fire. Huntress falls silent. Fox hesitates.*) I retract nothing! I'll add more!

FOX

I've never killed — a hound —

49

HOUND

Now I'm going to skin you foxy-woxy dearie booby baby pie! And wear you. Tease you. Tie you. And let you nose where others can't so easily — you know where!

FOX

(*raising the gun*) I KNOW WHAT TO DO!

HOUND

Remember the click?

FOX

Click?

HOUND

There are no live guns allowed in this hunt! Oh ho hahahaha! (*He leaps, lashing. Fox stumbles back and shrieks. The gun fires as Fox goes down. Hound staggers, incredulous. Huntress screams. Fox leaps up, throwing the gun away, dashing disjointedly in confused terror.*)

FOX

Oh foxmother, oh foxfather, oh my foxgod, oh my foxhood, oh foxchrist, oh foxbabies ohh — (*Huntress continues screaming, reaching hysteria as Fox dashes about the stage, trying to find a place to hide, ultimately trying to throw himself through the stage.*) Down the foxhole — down the dark hole — into the tunnel — any tunnel — any hole — down in the dark — any dark — deep in the hole — dark in the deep! dark! of the dark! and the deep! the deep! the deep! HOLE! (*He crouches by the broken wall in failure.*) And I won't — no I won't — NO I'LL NEVER COME OUT TO THE LIGHT SEE FOX HIDE HIDE FOX! (*Huntress climaxes. Fox jumps up, stares at her in an impotent, shaking rage, grabs the gun, and aims.*) You're nothing special either! Nothing as me! So shut up. It fired once, maybe it will fire AGAIN! (*Huntress is unafraid, intrigued, and glued to his words. She trails into silence. Confused.*) What am I doing . . (*He drops the gun, shaking.*) What have we done! (*He lowers his head, displaying the mask, rubbing his "eyes."*) No Hound. No Huntress! (*He raises his head and meets her glance. Blackout. The lights rise slowly on Fox, staring ahead, sitting on the wall. Huntress is on the stump — the crate. The manikin Hound and the gun lie between them.*) Want to talk?

HUNTRESS

No. (*pause*) Want to talk?

FOX

No. (*pause*) I won't let you near me again.

HUNTRESS

I'll have to kill you. (*slight pause*) It's the way I — I — have to — to get, to get . . (*slight pause*) I don't understand about the gun.

FOX

Me neither. (*pause*)

HUNTRESS

Some things are unpredictable.

FOX

Guns? (*pause*)

HUNTRESS

He was a nice hound.

FOX

He was in love with you.

HUNTRESS

Silly hound!

FOX

Look at him lying there!

HUNTRESS

That's what happens when you die.

FOX

I've seen death. Blood. Flesh. Bones. Other stuff. Not plastic!

HUNTRESS

You explain it. (*slight pause*)

FOX

You were hanging on the wall! (*Slight pause. Feeling a little foolish.*) I put you together.

HUNTRESS

That, maybe. (*She points to the manikin Hound.*) This, never. (*She points to herself.*)

FOX

I guess not . .

HUNTRESS

And he wasn't like that. Ohh noo . . (*She gestures at Hound. Pause.*)

FOX

I guess I don't understand.

HUNTRESS

(*sensual again*) Let it happen.

FOX

I'll see you a manikin again first! (*slight pause*) Or whatever.

51

HUNTRESS

Life's one long getting to —

FOX

Getting away —

HUNTRESS

To —

FOX

Away —

HUNTRESS

To!

FOX

Away away away rain rain go away — baby — wants to play — to play — (*agonized*) all the babies are dead, all laid to bed! (*pause*) Some things are mysteries. (*pause*) I saw the last fox babies.

HUNTRESS

Babies are cute.

FOX

They were my sister's. (*Pause. She waits for him to go on.*)

HUNTRESS

Were they — who was — their father? (*pause*) Ohh.

FOX

The Egyptians married their sisters: they even worshiped foxes!

HUNTRESS

Jackals.

FOX

(*slight pause*) We did the only thing possible then. That was right! And the babies — (*slight pause*)

HUNTRESS

Dead. (*pause*)

FOX

She disappeared. I was doing what I could.

HUNTRESS

Babies are cute.

FOX

Then some hunters — in blue — came into the alley — (*pause*) In a place called, jesus foxcrap, Hollywood! (*He laughs.*) The last fox and the last fox babies! (*more laughter*) The city was the only forest left! (*slight pause*) My stomach is full of lousy wine and my heart is hungry. (*slight pause*) They were all warm and curled and sleeping. And half-starved. I was a lousy father too! And the cops were coming, coming, coming! So I left. (*slight pause*) I slipped by them in a sweat down Hollywood Boulevard hoping a Food Giant truck would hit me. It was an AAA repair truck. (*pause*) I wish it had been fatal! (*pause*) So I got hold of myself and raced back to the alley and watched where they took them. (*pause*) To a laboratory.

HUNTRESS

A lav?

FOX

> Fox be nimble,
> Fox be quick,
> Baby jump over that scalpel
> QUICK!

(*pause*)

HUNTRESS

Babies are so nice to — touch —

FOX

Do you know what they were doing?

HUNTRESS

Experimenting! That's what they do in lavs! (*Fox stares at her, unable to fathom her reactions. He tries to reach her with his pain.*)

FOX

They were trying to find out what made a fox a fox. They were trying to find out what made us the way we are! (*slight pause*) They were trying to find out why a fox wasn't a man and why a man wasn't a fox. They were trying to find out whether we were even foxes. And they weren't even men! And they killed my babies! You could see our history stop! (*pause*) They didn't stop there. (*slight pause*) Why did a fox die? What made a dead fox? Why did a dead fox stay a fox? So they pulled them apart limb by organ by muscle by bone by sample by section by cell until there wasn't anything left but the memory of foxhood. And that tormented them! So they pulled themselves apart . . Arm by gut by muscle by . . (*slight pause*) Trying to get at their memory . . Their memory of why a fox should be that memory! Why that memory should be a fox! That memory! (*slight pause; explosively*) Why — I — should — be — . . WHY! (*pause*) A fox wants. A fox hungers. A fox thinks. See Fox run!

HUNTRESS

See Fox hide!

53

FOX

See Fox cry —

HUNTRESS

See Fox hide!

FOX

A fox is a hunted being —

HUNTRESS

See Fox hide!

FOX

Saddens —

HUNTRESS

Joys —

FOX

Bleeds —

HUNTRESS

Understands! (*pause*) Dies.

FOX

(*at a loss*) No Huntress no Huntress no Huntress no . . (*Blackout. Fox-hunt sounds reprise. They fade into laughter. Lights up on Fox and Huntress passing the bottle back and forth having a fine time, though whenever she tries to caress him, he pulls back. She's "on the make."*) I don't understand you all the time . .

HUNTRESS

It's a difficult hunt . . (*reacting to his pleased expression*) You're a terribly subtle fox . .

FOX

Not really . .

HUNTRESS

Really!

FOX

Well I think you're a great hunter.

HUNTRESS

Huntress.

FOX

You're a cute chick!

HUNTRESS

Not really . .

FOX

Yeah, I wouldn't say it if I didn't mean it.

HUNTRESS

You're a great guy too! (*He pulls away from her.*)

FOX

You don't mean it!

HUNTRESS

One hell of a man!
You know what I mean!

FOX

Not really —

HUNTRESS

Yesss . . (*They are laughing. Fox pulls sharply back from her caress.*)

HUNTRESS

Whatcha so nervous about, baby?

FOX

I won't let you get me!

HUNTRESS

I was before . .

FOX

That was then! (*slight pause; seductive, toying with her zipper*)

HUNTRESS

I can do it again.

FOX

(*laughing deprecatingly as she pulls it down a bit*) Oh ho ha no.

HUNTRESS

You can't keep your — eyes — off me!

FOX

Oh ho ha no. I mean yes! Haha, won't get me again!

HUNTRESS

Oh c'mon, foxy-doxy dearie, you've got a thing on for me! (*She pulls the zipper more, laughing. Fox is laughing, in fits, taking swigs, betraying nervousness, confusion, fascination, and — fear. Abruptly, almost throwing it, he thrusts the bottle on her, forcing her to leave the zipper alone.*)

FOX

Drink?!

HUNTRESS

Anything you say! (*manfully takes a swig*) Want me to dance for you? Think that would help? You should see me —

FOX

I don't need help!

55

HUNTRESS

Not everything's aimed to get you — relax! Enjoy life a little more! Everything works out for the best!

FOX

Yeah. Sure. (*She leans over and gives him a quick kiss and then pulls back herself, leaving him hanging.*)

HUNTRESS

Thererere . . That wasn't so bad, was it . .

FOX

Uh, no . .

HUNTRESS

So what's a little dancing then?

FOX

I don't know —

HUNTRESS

Where's your animal vitality. Where's your male daring? Can't you do ANYTHING, FOX?

FOX

Sure! Why not? Dance!

HUNTRESS

Just you watch!

FOX

Don't you need music?

HUNTRESS

(*stands and starts dancing, slowly, sensuously, indulging her body, building her excitement and rhythm*) Oh no, you just moove a little, moove, streeetch, get your rhyyythmmm, boop-de-doo, buuuiiild it — ahhh — ummmm — pant a little for me, Foxy! Excite me, you sly thing you you thing! (*Fox stares. She becomes wilder and freer.*) C'mon! Whatcha gotta lose by a little hot breathing!

FOX

Pant. Pant. I'm out of my mind.

HUNTRESS

I'M ONE HUGE GOOOOOSEBUMP!

FOX

Hahaha pantpantpantpantpantpantpant hahaha.

HUNTRESS

You too!

FOX

(*weakly*) I don't know how —

HUNTRESS

Just — let — it — all — out — react — dance — react — let — it — happen — good boy —react — to — me — to — me — to — me — there! Good! (*Fox starts: once underway, he takes his tensions out in it. Huntress is peaking.*) C'mon, Foxy dearie, let go let go let go let go let go wow! (*He lets go. He becomes wild. She abruptly stops and watches as he gets carried away. Coldly*) Let it all out, Fox. All that tension. All that fear. All that pressure. Let it go. Show it. Get weak! (*She repeats the "get weak" as a rhythmic chant until Fox is reduced to an uncontrollable shaking, groaning through his teeth. She assuredly closes on him, puts his hand on her zipper, and embraces him with a manufactured ardor.*)

FOX

Ohh. Ahh. Unnh. (*For a desperate moment he responds to her. She begins laughing, in control, winning. With a shudder he tears away. She wipes the taste of him off her lips.*) NO! Do you think I'm some sort of animal? (*She laughs coldly at him.*)

HUNTRESS

You're going to like licking yourself.

FOX

I remember Hound!

HUNTRESS

He needed that. Hound had to be excited, see? So we'd hunt — we could usually turn something up.

FOX

Forget it!

HUNTRESS

(*brutally*) A dead carcass under a Food Giant truck. (*Slight pause: his attention is riveted on her.*) One still a little alive from an AAA truck.

FOX

No . .

HUNTRESS

The last fox — sister — in a dark alley — (*slight pause*)

FOX

No.

HUNTRESS

Babies too.

FOX

YOU WEREN'T IN THE LABS!

HUNTRESS

Let go of me! (*Slight pause. He backs down.*) And nooow, the last fox. (*slight pause*) And once we'd turned something up, I'd chain Hound in his own need his own chain he'd I'd chain — (*slight pause*) His face would get so contorted! He was so sad. (*She laughs at his stare.*) He'd get so hot under the collar watching it all. What a dog. The Fox! And he'd break free — or I'd let him go — and then I'd take him —

FOX

HE TOOK YOU THE LAST TIME!

HUNTRESS

That was his last time.

FOX

Because I killed him!

HUNTRESS

But the gun had no bullets.

FOX

I fired!

HUNTRESS

(*broadly amused*) He was a manikin!

FOX

He died!

HUNTRESS

What a fantasy!

FOX

You're laughing at me!

HUNTRESS

I'm closing fast. Because the gun did fire. Fox did fire!

FOX

I keep thinking I've got you pegged, and then — (*Suddenly she leaps at him: he jumps. Thereafter she stalks him, comically, because of his prat-falls, though Fox is half out of his mind with fear and anticipation.*)

HUNTRESS

WHAM!! Out of left field!

FOX

Hey!

HUNTRESS

I'm a lot of women, Fox!

FOX, HOUND, & HUNTRESS

FOX
Too many!

HUNTRESS
We need a reckoning!

FOX
I'd rather subtract —

HUNTRESS
I'll get you for taking my hound away!

FOX
I'm sorry, so sorry, but it was some sort of accident —

HUNTRESS
I owe you something for getting rid of that hound!

FOX
I'm grateful you're grateful —

HUNTRESS
I'm going to wear you!

FOX
Oh no —

HUNTRESS
Tease you, tie you —

FOX
Let me unravel!

HUNTRESS
Let you poke where others can't so easily —

FOX
Stay away!

HUNTRESS
I'm going to tire you, sweetie!

FOX
That's for sure!

HUNTRESS
Trace your circlings —

FOX
You're an expert —

HUNTRESS
Make you a sad fox, sad face, contorted —

FOX
I'M ANGUISHED!

HUNTRESS

You'll get so hot under the collar —

FOX

Oh foxgod!

HUNTRESS

You'll be so happy —

FOX

I can't believe it!

HUNTRESS

I'll drive you to your den —

FOX

If only I had one —

HUNTRESS

(*closing*) Smoke you out. Smoke. SMOKE!

FOX

(*coughing, as if from smoke*) No — ah! Oh. Stay — ah! Back! Ahh!

HUNTRESS

Out into the light, Fox!

FOX

I won't come out for you!

HUNTRESS

WHERE I CAN TAKE YOU! (*She grabs him: he cries out.*) Bite you! Bleed you! Drag you! Into the open! Into the light! (*She makes love, violently.*) I'm going to expose you expose you expose every hair every limb every organ every muscle every bone every section every cell exalt you degrade you absorb absorb absorb you release you capture you give birth to you kill you leash you chain chain chain and hound you free you hunt with you hunt you circle you with me from every direction me me me me me me me me me me me me me me me me! (*Fox at first drowns in her, confused, stifled, wanting, despising. As her passion builds, he responds. As she climaxes, he struggles, finally bursting in desperation, loving her, hating her, seizing hold of her at the peak.*)

FOX

Ohh, no, yes, oh no, oh yes! No, no, noooo, yesss! No, oh! No! No! No! NO! YES! NOOOO!

HUNTRESS

Ahh! AHH!

FOX

Uhh! UHH! I — WON'T — LET — YOU — HAVE — MEEEEEEEE! (*They peak*

*together: at the summit he strangles her. She resists desperately, and col-
lapses. He pulls back, his mouth working, full of terror and horror, re-
leasing himself through a series of shudders culminating in a wordless
scream. Blackout. In the blackout, as the music fades, Fox's compulsive
chant of "No Hound! No Huntress!" is heard. His head is down to the
audience, swaying back and forth: he raises it, still chanting, and discovers the manikin that has replaced Huntress. The chant, after a beat,
turns to one of joy and release. In a burst he tears both manikins apart
and scatters the pieces. Then he cavorts in happiness.*) No Hound! No
Huntress! Fox alone! (*Pause. The excitement at length has drained. He
surveys the wreck of his hopes.*) No Hound. No Huntress. (*pause*) Fox.
Alone. (*Pause. He grabs for a modus operandi.*)

    "Before the pack for many a mile
    A fox had sped in gallant style —"

(*He breaks off.*) What pack. (*angry*) What dreams! (*anguished*) What
Fox . . What a hell of a hope! (*slight pause: flat confusion*) I loved
you, Hound. (*slight pause*) I loved you, Huntress. (*slight pause*) You
were something! (*slight pause*) I've gotta be crazy! (*He puts his head
down and shakes back and forth in anger, anguish. Chanting*) No
Hound. No Huntress. Crazy Hound. Crazy Huntress. No Hound! No
Huntress! Crazy Fox crazy Hound crazy Huntress no Hound no Huntress
no Fox no Fox no Fox NO Fox NO FOX! (*Pause: he slowly looks up.*)
NO HOUND! (*He laughs.*) NO HUNTRESS! (*He tears the mask off and flings
it upward.*) No Fox no man but free!

BLACKOUT

Fox, Hound, & Huntress by Lance Lee was first presented
on August 15, 1971 at the Odyssey Theatre in Los Angeles. It was directed by Geraldine Chiabrera.

Cast of Characters

FOX	Michael Pritchard
HOUND	Michael Steinberg
HUNTRESS	Susan Carne

W.E.R. LA FARGE

IN COLLABORATION WITH THE FIREHOUSE THEATER
COMPANY

Escape by Balloon

A THEATRE PIECE IN ELEVEN EVENTS

Cast of Characters

Between seven and twelve actors and musicians are required

ESCAPE BY BALLOON

A large, open room. In the center, a litter designed to carry two people facing each other in a sitting position. Around the litter sheets of white paper and pots of poster paint. Around the periphery of the room several platforms of various heights. One of these houses the two musicians. The others are used by the actors at various points throughout the evening. Later, a platform ten by twelve by two feet high will be constructed in the center of the space. The audience sits wherever they choose. No chairs are provided.

Event One
ROOTS

As the audience enters the space, each individual is confronted by an actor. The actor asks a series of questions designed to make the audience member aware of his roots (or lack of them) and to make him consider his own and his ancestors' westward journeys: "Were you born in California?" "Why did you come to California?" "Did you find what you are looking for?" "What was the hardest thing to leave behind?" "Why did your ancestors come to this country?" *Etc. (The questions may be modified according to the locale of the production.) While asking these ques-*

tions, the actor takes a gesture from the audience member. He may do this by asking for a nonverbal answer to one of his questions or by involving the audience member in some physical activity. This gesture will be used by the actor in a later event. The actor removes the audience member's shoes.

Event Two
RECOGNITION

During "Roots," two actors (male and female) search for a couple from the audience. When a willing couple is found, the actors explain to them that they will be a focus for the action throughout the evening. This couple will be recipients of the dreams and fears of the rest of the audience. They are invited to take off their clothes, to be as naked as possible, like sheets of blank paper. Whether or not the couple decides to be naked, they are seated in the center of the room on a specially constructed litter facing each other. Ponchos of white butcher paper are slipped over their heads and one of the couple is given a bowl of grapes or strawberries. They are instructed to feed the berries to one another in alternation. With the first berry the man reminds the woman of some happy, joyous event from their past. The woman does likewise. With his second berry, the man reminds the woman of some unhappy, disturbing event from their past. The woman does the same, and so on throughout this event. When the couple is in the center, all other actors begin to question the audience on the subject of the ideal relationship: "What constitutes an ideal relationship?" "What obstacles prevent an ideal relationship?" Etc. Audience members are instructed not to answer these questions verbally, but to express their thoughts and feelings by painting on the couple with the tempera paints available in the center. There are additional pieces of paper of various sizes and shapes from which the audience can fashion crowns, banners, etc. Everyone paints with his fingers. Finally, the couple is transformed into a colorful, messy work of art, in some way embodying whatever that particular audience collectively feels about the ideal relationship. Together, the actors and the audience create a new thing, a whole thing: the transformed couple. This new thing will have symbolic as well as actual significance in the successive events. When the painting is nearly complete, the actors, scattered throughout the audience, begin to sing.

ESCAPE BY BALLOON

Event Three
INVOCATION

ACTORS

Something sleeping,
Something new:
    A new place,
    A place waiting.
    A voice within me:
    When I answer, who am I?

Something empty,
Something full:
    A voice within me.

A new place,
A place waiting.

All new things:
Another time,
A new hour,
Unseen islands,
Wild weather:
An old place, waiting.

And a voice within me:
When I answer, who am I?

(*An actor interrupts the singing to address the audience. While he speaks, the others clear away the paints and leftover papers.*)

ACTOR

There was a boy once, who went to the wedding of two people who lived in his same village. He saw the couple: he saw their relationship. But he wanted to see more. So he followed them home to the place where they were to spend the night. He looked in through the window of the bedroom, and he saw them, the man and the woman. He saw them kneel down by the side of the bed, fold their hands, and begin to pray. And he felt at that moment that he was no longer the observer, but the observed.*

*The story of the boy who looks through the window is taken from "The Observed," a short story by Frank O'Connor, and is used with permission.

Nothing stays as it is. What's happened so far, we've all seen. Some things happen that no one sees. We're going to take this couple away now. You must stay here. We will report to you what is happening. (*The actors resume singing and carry the couple into an adjoining room.*)

Event Four

CONSUMMATION

Two actors engage the couple in a ceremony in the adjoining room. The rest of the actors bring the audience reports of what is happening, using the following lines. The lines are divided among the actors and spoken one at a time, more or less in the order given. To the beginning of his list of lines each actor adds one or two improvisational lines describing anything he sees or imagines happening in the adjoining room.

ACTORS

They are in the other room now.
They are sitting down.
They are catching their breath.
They are sitting facing each other.
They are talking quietly.
They are thinking noisily.
They are looking at each other.
She is saying: please don't look at me so intently.
She is remembering her grandmother.
He is remembering pioneers.
She is remembering hiding.
He is talking about Sunday afternoons.
She is remembering crying.
She is talking about her first-grade teacher.
He is thinking about salt water.
She is thinking about getting older.
She is talking about getting older.
He is seeing her grandmother.
She is remembering her father and mother.
He is talking about his uncle.
She is changing into her grandmother.
He is talking about a hired man.
She is thinking of the sun.
He is changing into his uncle.

She is changing into her aunt.
He is changing into flowers.
She is changing into scissors.
He is changing into rock.
She is changing into earth.
He is changing into water.
She is changing into his uncle.
He is changing into a potted pyrocanthus.
His grandfather, who is a tree, is waving his branches.
She is changing into fire.
She is changing into a landscape.
He is changing into rain.
She has changed into rock.
He has changed into lightning.
She has changed into the ocean.
He has changed into a whale.
She has changed into a mountain.
He has changed into a glacier.
She has changed into a harbor.
He has changed into a ship.
She has changed into an army.
He has changed into a citadel.
She has changed into a man.
He has changed into her mother.
She is picking him up.
He is putting her in his pocket.
She is tying him around her neck.
He is folding her down the middle.
She is zipping him up.
He is buttoning her down.
She is ironing him out.
He is tucking her in.
He is winding her up.
She is beside herself.
He is above himself.
She is slamming him shut.
She is putting him in order.
He is cutting her in small pieces.
He is putting his hand inside her.

She is putting him in her mouth.
He has jumped down her throat.
She swallowed him.
He is passing inside her like a pig in a python.
Her stomach is stretching: it's getting bigger and bigger.
She is changing into flowers.
She is saying the Our Father.
Her stomach is enormous.
She is spinning around and around, like the earth.
He is coming out between her legs.
She is changing into earth.
The force of her spinning is loosening her stomach.
He is coming out between her legs.
Her spinning has ripped him from her stomach, like a tide.
He is spinning around and around her, like the moon.
She is kneeling.
He is covered with wet hair, like a sea otter.
She is saying the Hail Mary, and her hands are smoking.
They are spinning around each other.
Flames are streaming from her fingertips.
The smoke is rising, like the stalk of a flower.
The smoke is licking the ceiling.
She is putting him in her pocket.
He is kneeling.
He is buttoning her up.
They are kneeling together.
White lines are streaming backwards from her body, like a person on a
    motorcycle.
White lines are streaming backwards from his body, like a person on a
    motorcycle.
His body is arching forward against the blast.
She is catapulting through time, ahead of herself.
He is vibrating to pieces.
She is quivering with energy.
The vibrations have multiplied his heads.
Her hands are straining to hold him together.
His vital organs are shaking beyond control.
She is being swallowed into the onrushing moment.
The shock wave is dividing his identity.

70

The speed of her travel has expanded her mass.
Time is speeding to a standstill.
They are here, elsewhere, and everywhere.
Her hair is streaming backwards.
His hair is streaming backwards.
White lines are streaming from her hair.
His face is flattened by the wind.
Her cheeks are flattened by the wind.
His eyes have water in them.
Her cheeks have water on them.
She is remembering her brother.
He is seeing her grandmother.
It's all over.
(*Meanwhile, in the adjoining room, the couple's paper garments are
stripped off and stuffed into two large cloth bags. The two stand facing
each other about ten feet apart, a small bottle of wine and two glasses
midway between them. Lengths of yarn are tied neck to neck, wrist to
wrist, ankle to ankle. They are instructed to pour the wine into the
glasses and drink without allowing any of the strings to go slack. When
the reporting is over, the strings are broken, the couple are clothed in
robes, and a flat top is fastened to the litter so the couple may lie on it.
Once on the litter, they are covered with a green cloth and carried, with
the bags, back into the main space.*)

MUSICIAN

It looks like they're sleeping, but they may only be resting. (*The litter is
set in the middle of the space and the actors kneel around it to sing.*)

ACTORS

> And the spirit moved on the face of the waters.
> And the land lay waiting
> > Under the rain, the long rain,
> The ground lay sleeping
> > Under the sea, the salt seas;
> Blue-green and turquoise were the dreams of islands,
> Lavender, cerulean the dreams of earth
> Scarlet with the hope of birds,
> > Under the rain,
> > Under the sea.
> And the spirit moved on the face of the waters.

71

W.E.R. LA FARGE

Event Five

DREAM OF THE WEST

CLOWN*

The Age of Discovery. The discoverers dream of the West.

(*The actors go among the audience. Each has one "Dream of the West" line, as well as a parallel line gathered from the audience during "Roots." These audience lines refer to the westward journeys of individual audience members or their ancestors: "I came to get a better job," "My grandparents were being persecuted by the Czar," etc. As the actors move among the audience, each speaking two lines in alternation, they collect items of clothing from audience members, garbing themselves in the most flamboyant way possible. The actors are discoverers about to depart for the New World. The audience members are those who remain behind, being charmed and coerced into contributing to the greater glory of the discoverers.*)

ACTORS

Beyond these islands is another island good and great, and full of folk. There is a river, the streams whereof make glad the city of God.

Aristotle says, between the end of Spain and the beginning of India is a small sea navigable in a few days.

Pliny says the sea is narrow.

Solomon and Jehoshaphat sent ships which brought back gold, silver, and ivory.

Seneca says an age will come when the ocean will loose his chains and a huge land lie revealed.

Powerful kingdoms, cities, and provinces, very noble, very rich in all things, abundant, very necessary to us.

The graves have not been opened for gold, the mines not broken with sledges, nor their Images pulled down out of their temples.

We shall go always a little further: it may be beyond that last blue mountain barred with snow.

We ever held it certain that going toward the sunset we would find what we desired.

*The character of the Clown or Fool moves through the evening mocking or offering obscene and grotesque parallels to the activities of the other actors in each event. He also identifies certain moments with an appropriate title, and in the tenth event, "Escape by Balloon," he plays the dog, Top.

Event Six

DISCOVERY

Having garbed themselves in the clothing of the audience, the actors gather on a platform at the periphery of the performance space.

CLOWN

The court of Ferdinand and Isabella of Spain at the close of the fifteenth century: the voyages sanctified. (*The actors kneel and address two audience members as the King and Queen of Spain.*)

ALL

Most Christian, most exalted
Excellent and mighty
King and Queen of the Spains
And of the islands of the sea:

FIRST ACTOR

In the present year I saw: the banners of your Highness' raised on the towers of Alhambra.

SECOND ACTOR

I saw: the Moorish kings come forth to the gates.

THIRD ACTOR

I saw: them kiss the hands of your Highnesses, and of my Lord, the Prince.

FOURTH ACTOR

I saw: a new map of the world.

FIFTH ACTOR

I saw: a book.

SECOND ACTOR

Powerful kingdoms, cities, and provinces.

SIXTH ACTOR

I saw: the name of the Grand Kahn, which means in our language King of Kings.

SEVENTH ACTOR

Who many times had sent for teachers, but the Holy Father never sent any to him.

FIRST ACTOR

Wherefore many cities were lost.

THIRD ACTOR

Wherefore your Highnesses sent me bearing Christ.

ALL

Wherefore your Highnesses sent me bearing Christ over the Sea.
(*Throughout this scene the discoverers are competing for the favor of the King and Queen. They sing out the last lines all together, at the same time reaching and grasping for the treasures of the New World. They are interrupted by the Clown.*)

CLOWN

The voyages. (*One by one the discoverers leave the platform and begin to circle the performance space at the periphery. As they move, they develop the gesture taken from an audience member in "Roots."*)

FIRST ACTOR

Blessed be the light of day
And the Holy Cross, we say.
Good is that which passeth,
Better that which cometh.

SECOND ACTOR

I saw: green weed: many bunches of green weed: weed from rocks: river weed: a sure sign of land.

THIRD ACTOR

I saw: a multitude of birds.
Birds flying westward.
A sign. A sign.
Two or three small birds singing.

FOURTH ACTOR

The sea very smooth like a river.
The sea flat and calm.
The sea like a river.
Air the best in the world.

FIFTH ACTOR

I saw: a great cloudbank: a drizzle without wind.
A great sign of land.
Many tuna: much more weed: a live crab.
A sign.

SIXTH ACTOR

I saw: a tern, two boobies, four boatswain birds.
A bird like a tern, a river not a sea bird.
Four boobies twice. A dove. A duck. A frigate bird.
A sign. A sign. A sure sign.

SEVENTH ACTOR

I saw: city of Heaven: Quinsay, Zaitun.
Islands of gold: Antillia,
Cippangu, San Borondon, St. Brendan's,
Santanaxia, Mayda, the Green Island,
Island of Demons, Brazil Rock,
Atlantis.

(*When all are circling, each speaking his discovery refrain, the circle tightens on the center, the refrains grow louder. As the circle comes close to the couple in the center the actors drop their individual refrains and all begin to chant.*)

ALL

A cane. A stick. A board. A plant.

(*They move faster and faster, their voices dropping to a whisper, until all freeze when one actor cries out.*)

FIRST ACTOR

A light. (*As each actor speaks his line in the following sequence, he turns to look at the couple.*) I saw: a light.

SECOND ACTOR

I saw: land.

THIRD ACTOR

A light.

FOURTH ACTOR

A little light.

FIFTH ACTOR

A light like a candle.

SIXTH ACTOR

I saw: a candle.

SEVENTH ACTOR

A wax candle.

SECOND and SIXTH ACTORS

A light.

THIRD and FIRST ACTORS

Land.

FIFTH ACTOR

A light like a candle.

SEVENTH ACTOR

A little wax candle.

75

FOURTH, FIFTH, and SECOND ACTORS

I saw: land.

SEVENTH ACTOR

A little wax candle rising and falling.

(*The actors speak the following lines as they approach the couple carefully.*)

DISCOVERERS

I saw: gold.

I saw: gold-bearing streams. River of Midas: gold-bearing streams.

I saw: pearl fisheries, precious stones, an island all gold.

I saw: gold, grains of paradise, pepper.

I saw: teeming cities, monsters of human kind.

I saw: elephants, parrots, gryphons, slaves.

I saw: dog-headed men.

I saw: naked people. Ambergris. Gold on a beach.

I saw: horn of the narwhal, the narwhal's potent horn.

I saw: a room full of gold.

I saw: secrets of the world.

I saw: seven cities.

I saw: spices and sugar, ivory, silk.

I saw: powerful kingdoms, cities, and provinces.

I saw: the manner of their conversion.

I saw: City of Heaven.

I saw

I saw

I saw

I saw

Event Seven
GREED

The discoverers open the bags of paper and pull out the contents. Filled with awe, they examine the colored paper while speaking the "I saw" lines. Gradually, they become possessive of the bits of paper, and each collects as much as he can for himself. The actors leave the central area and go out among the audience — three groups of two and one alone. Conflict develops over the paper, each of the three groups demonstrating an aspect or consequence of greed: physical violence; buying and selling; respect and affection in exchange for goods. The "I saw" lines evolve into nonverbal sounds. The lone actor stuffs paper into his costume, un-

til he is vastly inflated. By this time, the conflicts in the three groups have escalated out of control. The stuffed actor picks up a small bell and signals to the musicians. The musicians begin to play and sing "Adoramus Te." The stuffed actor has become the Pope. With the Clown as attendant, the Pope goes among the quarreling groups, silencing their conflicts and taking most of their paper. The Clown continues to stuff the Pope with this paper until he is grotesquely huge. The Pope gathers all his followers around the prone couple and rings his bell for attention.

CLOWN

Fourteen ninety-four: Pope Alexander VI divides the world between Spain and Portugal. (*The following speech is spoken in nonsense Latin by the Pope and translated by the Clown.*)

POPE

Fabricando et construendo unam lineam a polo Artico scillicet Septemtrione ad polem antarticum Episcopus Romanus consessit et donavit Castelle regibus et suis successoribus regiones et Insulas novi orbis in Oceano occidentali Hispanorum navigationibus repertas.

Nulli ero omineum hominum liceat si quis autem hoc attentare praesumpserit indignatione Omnipoententem Dei.

Patris et Filli et Spiritus Amen.

CLOWN

Drawing a line, north and south, from pole to pole on the said ocean sea: a perpetual mark, unable to deny it or erase it or remove it at any time, in any manner, forever and ever.

What God has put asunder, what man dares join?

(*The Pope distributes the couple and their robes to the actors. All sing "Adoramus Te" as the couple's robes are torn off and they are brutally separated. One actor takes one of the couple to a platform on one side of the room, another actor takes the other to a platform on the opposite side. For a few moments all glory in their possessions, then "Adoramus" stops abruptly and there is silence.*)

Event Eight

THE PURITANS

There is a sudden turning. The actors turn from their greed with a cry and a gesture of penitence. All return to the center where they strip off their elegant clothes commandeered from the audience and blindfold themselves.

CLOWN

The beginning of the seventeenth century: The Puritans come to America. (*The blindfolded actors move toward the periphery of the room singing.*) "Wee shall be as a citty upon a Hill, the eies of all people are uppon us; soe that if wee shall deale falsely with our god in this worke wee have undertaken and so cause him to withdrawe his present help from us, wee shall be made a story and a byword through the world."*

Event Nine

ABSENCE OF THE FATHERS

All the actors are at the periphery of the room. The singing stops.

CLOWN

The end of the eighteenth century: The Fathers build a new nation. (*The Fathers move toward the center, still blindfolded, calling to each other. Each actor has several lines distributed throughout the following text. These lines are scored into a song, but the song is not sung straight through. Instead, the lines come in the order indicated, which means that each song is interrupted by the others. When one actor reaches another in the center they remove each other's blindfolds. At this point the somewhat tentative behavior imposed by blindness gives way to an authoritative stance. By the time the first section is over, all the actors have become Fathers, addressing the audience with full consciousness of their authority.*)

FATHERS

You didn't know us at first.
You didn't know who we were:
Not knowing our faces:
Never having seen us.
You didn't know our names.
You didn't know us.
There was a time you didn't know us.
You didn't know our faces:
Not knowing our names.
We were people. You, learning our faces.

*John Winthrop's sermon aboard the *Arbella*, spring 1630.

ESCAPE BY BALLOON

There was a time when we were people.
People to each other: people to people.
We didn't know each other.
You didn't know us.
We didn't know you.
We didn't know ourselves.
There was a time when we were people:
You, learning our names.
Bodies among other bodies:
Bodies with names. Bodies with faces:
Faces with eyes, growing beards. Deeds.
Children once:
Our parents didn't know us,
Knowing only our names.
Knowing only our faces.
Not knowing us. Not knowing who we were.
Knowing only our names.
You didn't know us.
Wc didn't know you.
We didn't know ourselves:
Learning each other's names:
People to people, learning names.
We didn't know who we were.
We knew our names, but our names were names:
Like other growing things.
Our faces were unfamiliar. Unfamiliar our deeds.
You didn't know us.
(*The Fathers leave the center and go out among the audience to recruit
help for building the stage which will be used for the last event. The
components of the stage are distributed about the room, and each actor
selects two audience members to help with the construction. During this
section only the indicated lines are used to give instructions — there is no
ad-lib instructing. While all actors but one supervise the building, the
remaining actor goes to a high place in the room to call roll.*)

FIRST ACTOR	FATHERS
Caesar Rodney	Men doing.
William Prescott	Men and women acting.
Thomas Knowlton	Taking responsibility.
Richard Gridley	Making plans.

79

Joseph Warren	Men thinking. Talking to others.
Thomas McKean	Men and women wondering.
Edward Rutledge	Thinking about what they hear.
Israel Putnam	Hearing about it. Thinking about it.
James Otis	Talking about it: wondering.
Robert Paine	Writing letters.
Josiah Quincy	Keeping order: the ones who keep order.
Stephen Hopkins	Working: the ones who work.
Charles Thomson	Making order.
John Sullivan	Standing: the ones who stand. Tall men
Peyton Randolph	and women: mothers and fathers.
Henry Knox	Taking risks. Risking your life. Making
Samuel Adams	plans. Planning.
Nathaniel Greene	Making things grow: wondering about
William Washington	growing: making plans. Keeping a garden.
George Mason	Men and women wondering: writing let-
Henry Lee	ters: being angry.
Artemas Ward	Not sleeping.
Robert Morris	Keeping a garden and not sleeping.
Haym Solomon	The ones who are tall. The ones who
Roger Sherman	move in houses: swaying slowly in kitch- ens. Mending: the ones who mend.
John Adams	Men and women acting.
Patrick Henry	Writing letters. Talking and not being
John Jay	heard: making protests: keeping a garden.
George Clark	Taking responsibility. The ones who stand.
Thomas Jefferson	Traveling: being away from home. Mak-
James Madison	ing resolves.
James Monroe	Writing proclamations. Arguing.
Benjamin Franklin	Men talking to men. Men and women
George Washington	writing.
(additional names ad lib)	Writing the Declaration of Independence. Standing: the ones who stand. Risking life and keeping gardens.
	Being ready.

Saying goodbye. Being angry. Saying goodbye.

Saying goodbye to gardens.

Men and women wondering.

Fighting and losing. Making laws. Fighting and losing. Making a government. Risking life. Taking command.

Losing and wondering: being ready. Men talking to men.

Men and women writing.

Fighting and winning. Making a nation.

Men and women acting.

(When the building is complete, the actor who called the roll and another actor sing a duet. The rest of the actors speak to small groups of audience members, using words from the text of the song.)

TWO ACTORS

Names known
Work done
Land begun:
Rest.
Leaving it to others.

You, learning.
Learning the names.
Not knowing: learning to know. Knowing.
Learning to know the names.

Risks run
Work done
Land begun:
Rest.

Leaving it to others.
Leaving it to you.
You, not knowing.
You, without names.
You, learning.
Learning to know: the ones who learn.
Knowing our names: your names not known.
You, learning.

Leaving it to you.
Not knowing your names.
Not knowing who you are.
Not knowing your faces.
Leaving it to you.

ALL

(*singing*) It is time to go.

ALL

(*singing and speaking*)

. . I, John Madison, being somewhat unwell but of sound disposing
mind and memory . .
. . being well advanced in years . .
. . remembering the mortality of this my body . .
I . . In the name of God, Amen.
. . this instrument, in writing . .
. . I, George Washington . .
. . I, Roger Sherman . .
. . I, James Monroe . .
. . give and bequeath . .
. . a sound disposing mind and memory . .
. . all my land . .
. . having recently been unwell . .
. . the land which lies by the river . .
. . being well advanced in years . .
. . that land on the far side . .
. . the land . .
. . all that land . .
. . the land which lies . .
. . the land . .
. . all the land . .
. . my land . .
. . all that land . .
. . the land . .
. . the land . .

It is time to go.
Those were good times:
Taking responsibility. Making plans. Fighting and losing.
God damn it.
Saying goodbye. Making order. Being ready. Arguing.

Men and women.
It was good.

It is time to go.
We don't know where.
Another life. A new task. Nothing.
To a rest. To a judgment. To a life.
To a task. To all. To zero.
Men talking to men.

Goodbye.
(*They climb up and leave, speaking until they are gone.*)
THE LAST ONE
Still angry,
Unwilling to go.
Not trusting. Not ready,
Still curious.
It was good.
God damn it.
(*Someone reaches down and pulls him up.*)
God damn it.

Event Ten

THE ESCAPE, BY BALLOON, FROM
RICHMOND: 1865*

The lights have faded during the preceding scene. In the dark the Clown speaks.

CLOWN
What the fathers had intended
Very soon was ended.
Civil war erupted,
Psyches were corrupted,
The union was distended.
Hardly a man is still alive

*Adapted from portions of *L'Ile Mysterieuse* by Jules Verne. The numbers in parentheses at the left of speeches indicate material within that episode which is spoken simultaneously. When speeches are being given simultaneously, focus is usually on one or else shifts back and forth. When an actor's material is not intended to be the center of focus, he chooses words and phrases to support and counterpoint the other actor. Where entire speeches are intended to be used in this way, they are marked by a dagger (†).

83

Recalling eighteen sixty and five,
When five determined men (and a dog)
Made good their escape by balloon from Richmond.
(*Someone enters with a flashlight, shining it on the stage, the audience, the walls. The actor with the light mounts the square stage in the middle of the space.*)
1. *Enter Pencroff. From one side of the room comes a voice. The flashlight picks out Pencroff.*

PENCROFF

Pencroff here. Pencroff. Sailor. American. Of the north. Twelve times around the world, me. It was I saw the balloon. I saw it: Pencroff. Slammed by the wind. Held fast. I stopped Cyrus Smith in the street. He didn't know me. I said: have you had enough of Richmond? I said: have you had enough of Richmond?
2. *Enter Spillett. From across the room comes a second voice. The flashlight swings to illuminate Spillett.*

SPILLETT

(2)   Gideon Spillett. Reporter, writer. I look, and looking, see. I write what I see, so that you, not seeing, may not live in darkness. My eyes are lanterns, blazing ahead through night.

PENCROFF†

(2)   He didn't know me. I saw the balloon. Slammed by the wind. Held fast. Slammed and banged and slammed by the wind. Held to the ground. Cabled fast. Banged and slammed and held fast.
(*duet of Spillett and Pencroff*)

PENCROFF	SPILLETT
	I see what is happening.
The rebels made it.	
	I see it before it is happening.
They to escape the siege of Grant.	
	I see it only beginning.
But the wind, the wind, the wind.	
	Beginning to happen.
God made the wind.	
	I see it taking place.
The hurricane is too much for them, I said.	

† Speeches from which the actor chooses words and phrases to counterpoint another actor's speech, which should receive primary attention.

I said: the wind will make us free.

The rebels made it, they to escape, but the wind, God made the wind. The hurricane is too much for them, I said. I said: the wind will make us free.

I see it stopping, going away.

I see it beginning, I see it only beginning, I see it before it is happening, I see it taking shape, I see it happening. Exact information from the center.

SPILLETT

(2)   These are the last words I wrote on my pad before being captured: "A rebel infantryman is drawing a bead on me right now." Poor devil. He missed. I made a sketch of him. He could not see what was happening. His bullet caved in darkness. My words leap into light. We are going somewhere, friends. Cyrus Smith stopped me in the street: he said: will you come with us, in a balloon? We are going somewhere, friends, we have nothing to risk but our lives.

PENCROFF†

(2)   Have you had enough of Richmond? I said: the wind. I said: the wind. Slammed on the ground. Tied down, cabled fast, slammed and banged and slammed by the wind. Held to the earth: God made the wind. I said: the wind. I stopped Cyrus Smith in the street. He didn't know me. I had seen the balloon. I said: Have you had enough of Richmond? I said: the wind will make us free.

3. *Enter Neb. From a third point in the dark room comes a voice.*

NEB

(3)   Nebuchadnezzar. Son of slaves. Born free. Free by my master, free by Cyrus Smith. Free to love him. Free to follow him. Free to die for him, prisoner of prisoners. I followed him to war. I followed him prisoner to Richmond. Richmond prisoner to Grant, Grant prisoner to his own guns. How does a son of slaves go through the lines, through the circles of prisoners, to his master, prisoner of prisoners? He is free.

SPILLETT†

(3)   I look, and looking, see. I write what I see, so that you, not seeing, may not live in darkness. I write what I see: exact information. Looking, seeing. You, not seeing. You, not knowing. I see what is happening. I see it before it is happening. I see it only beginning, beginning to begin. I see it happening. You, not seeing. My eyes are beacons, reaching forward, into darkness. I am the lighthouse on the shore. I watch the rocks. Exact information from the center. I talk of channels.

PENCROFF†

(3)   Twelve times around the world: Pencroff. American. Sailor. Of the north, of course. It was I saw the balloon. Held in Richmond, bound to escape. I said: can a man fly? Can a man ride one of these on the wind? Have you had enough of Richmond? He said: yes. He said: yes. I said: the wind. He said: yes.

4. *Enter Herbert. From a fourth point in the darkness comes a voice.*

HERBERT

(4)   Herbert Brown. A boy, a boy in the middle of the night. A boy in the rain. A boy with men. I'm going to hustle. Which is mine?

NEB†

(4)   Free to love him. Free to find him. Free to follow him. Free to live for him, prisoner of prisoners.

(*Spillett and Pencroff also continue in episode 4.*)

5. *Quartet. They come together. As each hears his name called by another he answers. The answers for each of them follow.*

PENCROFF

(*twice*) Filthy weather. (*last time*) Yes.

NEB

(*three times*) Good. Good.

HERBERT

(*three times*) Yes.

(*All speak together in the dark. Most lines are delivered only to the nearest of the audience. They call out to each other across the room.*)

PENCROFF

(5)   Tied down. Slammed by the wind. Every day. Held in Richmond, bound to escape. Spillett? Waiting. Waiting. Tied down. Banged by the wind. Worse every day. I said: can a man fly? Can a man ride one of these on the wind? Neb? Banged and torn and banged and torn. Tied down, slammed by the wind. Herbert? Waiting, waiting. Worse every day. Yes. Yes. Yes. Yes.

SPILLETT

(5)   Knowing, seeing, writing. Looking, writing. Knowing. We are going somewhere, friends. We are going somewhere, we have nothing to risk but our lives. Pencroff? We risk only our lives. Exact information from the center. Herbert? Knowing, seeing, writing. Looking, seeing, telling, knowing. We have nothing to lose but our lives. Neb? A man can do it. Yes. We are going somewhere, you will be with me, seeing, telling, understanding, knowing. Yes. Yes. Yes. Yes.

HERBERT

(5)   It's happening. It's happening. Someone is doing it. Right now. It's bursting, it's exploding. Somewhere I have never been, something I'm missing. I'm going to hustle. Which is mine? Neb? As I go running, wondering, hot and staring. He is putting the map in his pocket. He is putting the land in his pocket. Which is mine? Which is mine? I'm going to hustle. Pencroff? He is there, he is there. He is digging, he is tunneling, he is managing, he is acting, he is knowing the land, he is spinning his fingers away, away. As I go running, wondering, hot and staring, I'm going to hustle. Spillett? Which is mine?

NEB

(5)   Herbert? The master is prisoner: the slave is free. The son of slaves goes through the lines: Grant prisoner, Richmond prisoner, Cyrus Smith prisoner. Circle of prisoners: the son of slaves. Pencroff? The son is free. Son of slaves: free to find him, prisoner of prisoners. Free to follow him, prisoner of prisoners. Spillett? Free to free him, prisoner of prisoners. Yes. Yes. Yes. Yes.

6. *Enter Cyrus Smith. The four gather around the stage, each on a side. They develop a rhythmic chorus of "Yes." The lights come up on the stage to reveal Smith.*

SMITH

Cyrus Smith. Engineer. Prisoner of war. Free this evening.

7. *They are glad. This is what they say, intensely, but almost whispering, under the dialogue.*

SPILLETT

(7)   Knowing. Seeing. Telling. Writing. Yes. Yes. Looking, sketching, forming, seeing, understanding. Yes. Yes.

PENCROFF

(7)   Twelve times around the world. Yes. I said: the wind. Yes. The wind. Yes. The wind.

NEB

(7)   Free to love him. Good. Good. Free to find him. Good. Free to serve him. Good.

HERBERT

(7)   A boy with rain in his face. A boy in the wind. A boy with men. Yes, yes. Waiting to hear his name.

SMITH

(7)   I said, yes.

In the name of God: a man can do it.

87

To the other side of the lines.
To Ulysses Grant.
A man can do it.
(*One by one Smith brings the men onto the stage.*)
No damage to the balloon, Pencroff?

PENCROFF

I said: can a man ride one of these on the wind?

SMITH

I said: yes.
No damage, Pencroff?

PENCROFF

In a storm?

SMITH

Yes.

PENCROFF

In a hurricane?

SMITH

Yes.
No damage, Pencroff?

PENCROFF

(7)   No damage.
Banged and slammed and torn by
the wind. Held to the ground.
Waiting.

SMITH

(7)   Thank God. Tied down,
held to the ground. Banged and
slammed and torn by the wind.
Neb?

NEB

Yes.

SMITH

Spillett?

SPILLETT

Yes.

SMITH

Herbert?

HERBERT

Yes. Yes.

SMITH

No guard? No rebels?

SPILLETT

No guard. No rebels.

SMITH

They don't see what is happening. They don't see. Then we leave. Take places. Pencroff: cast off the ballast.

8. *First Casting Off. The five leap from the stage into the audience.*

CLOWN

Considering all that's been enacted heretofore,
The actors leave their characters behind
And struggle to apply the metaphor
To their own lives, and your lives, and mine.
How to keep our upside-down, high-flying, air-swimming selves aloft?
How to cast that load of personal ballast off?

(*One by one, each of the actors engages some members of the audience in an improvisational situation which illustrates something the actor would like to or is trying to cast off. An exploration of the limitations that prevent the full development of our human potential. As each actor returns to the stage after his casting off, he speaks.*)

FIRST ACTOR

Four to go.

SECOND ACTOR

Three to go.

THIRD ACTOR

Two to go.

FOURTH ACTOR

One to go. One more. (*When the last actor returns, they lock arms in the center of the stage in a circle, facing the audience.*)

SMITH

Ready cable.

PENCROFF

Cable ready.

9. *Enter Top.*

NEB

Here's Top.

PENCROFF

Top.

SMITH

Damn. Damn animal. Can't come now.

HERBERT

Top. Top, good boy.

PENCROFF

Here, boy. Come, Top.

NEB

Down. Down, boy.

PENCROFF

Slipped his collar.

SMITH

Down. Down, Top. Down, boy.

No room for you.

HERBERT

Oh, let him come. Please let him come.

PENCROFF

One more won't matter.

One more won't hurt. (*Pencroff lifts Top in. He perches on top of the circle.*)

SMITH

Cast cable.

PENCROFF

Cable cast. Now.

We're off.

10. *They ascend.*

SPILLETT

(10) I see it.

    I see it.

    Man flies.

    It is happening.

    He is riding the wind.

    I see it. I see it.

    Man prevailing.

    I see it happening.

    Man flying.

    Man ascending.

    Man seeing.

    Man. Man. Man.

    Man.

PENCROFF

(10) Now.

    Now.

    Now.

Now.
Wonder: man flies.
Wonder: he does it.
He tames the wind.
He knows how.
Man flies.
Now.
Now.
Now, he does it.
Now, he knows.

HERBERT

(10)   In a storm
In the wind.
At last.
Rising.
Rising.
He knows how.
Past roofs.
Past chimneys.
Rising, rising.
In the rain, rising.
In the wind, rising.
Man, rising.

SMITH

(10)   In the name of God:
A man can do it.
In the name of freedom:
A man can do it.
In the name of courage:
A man can do it.
In the name of science:
A man can do it.
In the name of his country:
A man can do it.

NEB

(10)   Leaving the ground, going upward away from the pavement
and hard soil. He does it, oh Lord: he is taking us upward away from
the ground in sliding mist, swinging away from floors and walls and upright solid things to touch.

91

11. *They are flying, still ascending.*

HERBERT

(11)   Herbert Brown. Herbert Brown. A boy, a boy. Herbert Brown. Herbert Brown.

PENCROFF

(11)   Pencroff. Pencroff. Pencroff. Sailor. Pencroff. Twelve times: Pencroff. Pencroff.

SPILLETT

(11)   I, Gideon Spillett. Gideon Spillett, reporter. I write what I see. Gideon Spillett. Gideon Spillett.

SMITH

(11)   Cyrus Smith. Cyrus Smith. Cyrus Smith. Engineer. Cyrus Smith.

NEB

(11)   Lord Jesus Christ, King of the universe.

12. *Flight. Each character is on his own flight — a fantasy of achievement and personal glory. Each sings a flight song, the text of which is chosen by the actor from a longer text. These longer texts are printed in the Supplementary Material following the play.*

SMITH

(12)   Who dost promise that when two or three are gathered together in thy name thou wilt grant their requests. Column of air pressing pressing our feet. Gas leaking. (*As Smith sings his flight song, he touches each of the others in some particular way. The others use this touch to develop a movement. Finally, all are moving together, a smoothly functioning organism given life by Smith.*)

PENCROFF

(12)   It was I saw the balloon. (*Pencroff stretches out on the floor of the stage. As he sings, the others raise him to a standing position as if he were a heroic statue. When he reaches the end of his song and a standing position, he performs a back flip.*)

>   They said it will not do,
>   It cannot do,
>   It's impossible it should do.
>   Won't do,
>   Can't do,
>   Never could,
>   Never does,
>   Never did do.

If it could have done
It would have done already.

(*After each of the flight songs, Smith interrupts to recall the character from his fantasy and draw attention to the perils of the situation.*)

SMITH

(12)   Direction unknown. Speed and altitude unknown. Time unknown.

SPILLETT

(12)
    I look, and looking, see,
    I see man like a king
    Ascending his throne.
    He is enthroned in the winds.
    Yes, he mounts the hurricane,
    The equinoctial storm.
    He knows how. He knows how.
    He saw the secrets.
    It was the work of his hands,
    His own hands.
    Nature gave over,
    Gave up her mysteries
    To the work of his hands
    And his all seeing eyes.
    Her secret fluids,
    Her currents,
    Her courses, winds, and mysteries.

(*As Spillett sings, he directs the others to form a human structure. Spillett climbs this structure, finally arriving on Pencroff's shoulders.*)

SMITH

(12)   (*bringing Spillett down*) Latitude and longitude, day or night, no sense of motion. Clouds moving, like ourselves. Wisps moving past, passing. Us passing wisps moving. Our own motion. Not rising. Moving past.

HERBERT

(12)   He is putting it in his pocket. (*As Herbert sings, he goes from one character to another. Each gives him some gesture, which Herbert expands and develops into a dance.*)

    I'm going to live longer than any.
    Someone is doing it right now.
    It's bursting, it's exploding.

He is putting the land in his pocket.
I'm going to hustle, which is mine?
Somewhere I have never been,
I'm going to live longer than any.

If I could reach my hands beyond my hands,
If I could stretch my arms beyond my arms.
As I go running, wondering, hot and staring,
I'm going to hustle, which is mine?
Somewhere I have never been,
I'm going to live longer than any.

SMITH

(12)   (*stopping Herbert*) Each other, moving in relation to each other. Pass, passing. No sense of moving, but we are moving.

TOP

(12)   (*Top's song is nonverbal. At the beginning of his song, all the other characters stand on their heads or shoulders. One by one, Top pushes them over. When they are pushed over, they begin to investigate one another using only the sense of smell. When an actor discovers a new smell, he begins to make little leaps from the prone or hands and knees position that he is in at the time. By the end of the song, all are leaping in unison.*)

SMITH

(12)   (*stopping Top*) Slipping past them passing us. Wisps going by. Not rising. Gas escaping, gas leaking. Over the land his own hands.

NEB

(12)   Take me where the finder loses and the loser keeps. More joy in heaven for the slow than the fast. (*As Neb speaks, all the others gather together on their knees for his sermon. As he sings, some of his lines and gestures are echoed and developed by this congregation.*)

In the storm, Lord, in the windy sea:
He's the One whose service makes you free.

Now the Lord said, Jonah, get up, go preach my people and pray:
He ran as fast as he could go the other way.

In the storm, Lord, in the windy sea:
He's the One whose service makes you free.

Now I've been down to the bottom of the sea,
Where the dark and the deep closed in and the weed wrapped round
    my skull.

Now you people of Ninevay you're living too red, white, and blue,
Your lying vanity's going to come back on you.
You'll be swallowed like Babylon, like Jonah in the tale,
In your high-flying, upside-down, air-swimming whale.

In the storm, Lord, in the windy sea:
He's the One whose service makes you free.

(*Neb brings his sermon to a close. Suddenly, all begin to perform their flight songs and flight activities at the same time.*)

13. *Not rising.*

SMITH

Pencroff! (*All freeze.*) Pencroff, are we rising, do you think?

PENCROFF

No, Captain, we're not rising. Worse than that.

SMITH

(13) Then cast off, Pencroff.
    The sensibility of balloons is well known.
    The slightest object, the right ounce:
    It is written in numbers: you may depend on it.
    It is justice, mathematical justice:
    You may hold on to it, Pencroff.
    Find the ounce! The right ounce.
    Balloons are famous for their equilibrium.
    You may depend on it, Pencroff.
    Throw over the weapons.
    Throw out the supplies.
    Throw everything that weighs:
    Guns, ammunition, tools, boxes.
    Cast off!

(*During Smith's speech, the others express their panic in brief fragments. All except Smith are huddled together, their words coming in short bursts, their movements aborted explosions. Smith stands alone, moving and speaking with smooth self-assurance.*)

OTHERS

(13) Gas going.
    Losing gas.
    Leaking. Escaping.
    Rent and torn. Turned over. Growing smaller.
    Gas escaping. Rushing.
    Not rising. Slipping. The air. Feet falling:

not touching: dropping: space under, no pressing:
tipping: empty, unsteady, sliding, down. Not touching.
Hold on.

(*When Smith reaches the end of his speech, all repeat "Cast off" to-gether and leap from the stage.*)

14. *Second Casting Off. The form for this is the same as for the First Casting Off, except all present their material at once, each to a different section of the audience. Not enough was cast off the first time. More needs to be cast off now. When each finishes his casting off he stands among the audience, waiting. When all are through, they rush to the center and leap onto the stage.*

15. *They accept the sea.*

PENCROFF

They are all thrown over, Captain.

SMITH

Are we rising, do you think?

PENCROFF

No, Captain, we are not rising. Worse than that, we're falling.

(*Quietly, simply, they speak to one another and to the audience.*)

SMITH

(15)   Slipping sideways.
        Yes. Always the same.
        Deep, giddy gliding.
        They don't see what's
        happening.
        Yes.

PENCROFF

(15)   The sea is not kind.
        Five determined men.
        We are facing it.
        In the name of freedom.
        In the name of man.
        A man can do it.

SPILLETT

(15)   All right, then.
        We face it. Good.
        We will do what men have to do.
        We are facing it.

96

HERBERT

(15)   Yes, the sea, we face it.
           We will do what men can do.
           All right then.

NEB

(15)   In the name of God.
           The endless plain.
           All right.
           Deep, giddy gliding.
           All right.

16. *Plunged in the sea. Simply, silently, they leave the stage. They walk among the audience. They bring nothing — no character, no performance. They search for some gift from the audience — a smile, a gesture, a look. When an actor gets some spark from an audience member, he develops that very specific look or gesture into a movement. For a moment he stays with the audience member, developing his movement, then he returns to the stage. Finally, all are onstage developing movements gathered from the audience. They exchange and extend these movements — a wild, foolish, gleeful dance.*

SMITH

(16)   Yes, we are rising. Yes.
           Softly pressing our feet.
           Lifting.
           Almighty God, who does promise that when two or three are gathered together in thy name . . grant their requests . . most expedient for them . . in this world knowledge . . in the world to come life . . Amen.

PENCROFF

(16)   We're rising. Like a sail, lifting us up.

SPILLETT

(16)   We're rising.
           Swinging upward and outward in the soft air.
           Five determined men.

HERBERT

(16)   We're rising.
           I'm going to live.
           I'm going to live longer than any.
           Longer. Longer.

The bells: ringing.
Guns booming.

NEB

(16)   We're rising. The wind is lifting us like a sail.
The wind is lifting us up,
The wind is lifting us upward and outward.

17. *The long moment. Now comes a moment of desolate, limp drifting.
They are hanging on. They are tired: it seems to go on and on. The
dance of episode 16 gradually slows down, until the actors are frozen in
position. They speak isolated words and phrases from earlier material,
but without any sense of triumph. This is simply endurance. Long pauses
between words. Only Top is mobile, moving around among the frozen
figures, searching the audience for a sign.*

18. *Land and falling. Finally, Top identifies someone in the audience
as land. He emits a loud squeal or cry. The cry releases the others from
their frozen positions. The six characters form two trios — Herbert, Smith,
Top; and Spillett, Pencroff, Neb. The two trios move from one side of
the stage to another, addressing the audience.*

HERBERT and SMITH

(18)   Top smells something.
What is it, Top?
What is it, boy?
He smells something.
He smells land.
All right, Top.
It must be land.
He's pointing.
All right.
It's land.
Might be an island.
Might be a continent.
Might be an island in the middle of the ocean.
Or a continent.
Can't see.
In the dark.
In the mist.

PENCROFF and NEB   SPILLETT

(18)   The wind is dropping.   (18)   No, it's not.
Look: it's collapsing.   Here it comes.

It's not filling.	No, it's filling.
It's not pressing out.	See, it's filling.
It's flapping, it's fluttering.	It's pressing out.
It's collapsing.	It's doing all right.
There's no gas left.	It's flapping a little.
It's caving in.	See. It's rising.
It's dropping. Sliding.	Now. It's filling.
Falling. Easy!	Filling a little.
Where is the wind?	Come on, now.
Going out. It's falling.	Where is the wind?
Whoa!	Where is the wind?
It won't come. It won't come.	Why not?
Easy, falling, slipping away.	Why?
Back in the sea!	

19. *Back in the sea. On Neb's line, "Back in the sea," the six come to-gether in a clump. At this point, all movement to the blackout is in slow motion. Slowly, Smith and Top are pulled away from the others and fall off into the sea.*

NEB

(*singing*) And Jonah woke up in a temple or a jail,
Round him were the bars and flying buttress of a whale.
You folks better watch out laying your track and your steel.
Because the machine's going to run you under its wheel.
You'll be swallowed . .
(*While Neb sings, the others accompany him with the chorus from his sermon.*)

OTHERS

In the storm, Lord, in the windy sea:
He's the One whose service makes you free.

20. *End of the flight. The last part of the flight is a weaving of four songs, taken from the two canons below. When Smith and Top finally fall off, Spillett cries out and all come abruptly to their knees. The slow motion resumes as the four remaining men rise to their feet and then begin to roll about the stage. The physical movement remains extremely slow, while the pace of the songs increases until the men fall from the stage. During this section the lights fade to black.*

PENCROFF and HERBERT

Canon I

(20)   Rising again. Why? Why? I don't know why. I don't know.

99

I only know: rising. Holding. Dragging upward. Pulling up. In the dark. My hands holding. Yes. Yes. Holding. Hands aching. In the name of God: a man can do it. Why? I don't know. Fingers aching. I don't know why. Two or three gathered together. In the dark. Hands holding. Aching. With one accord. Aching. In the name of science. Rising and falling, hands holding. In the name of freedom. A man can do it. Yes. Through mist, in the dark. Why? I don't know why. I only know: falling gently, hands holding. I don't know why. I don't know why . .

SPILLETT and NEB

Canon II

(20)   Yes. Yes. We will endure. Yes: endure, squeezing. Once again, hanging on. Yes. He will survive, hands holding, once again, squeezing the ropes, 'til it takes him, rising and falling, weaving down through the air, cross breezes and currents, hands holding, through the mist, rising and falling gently, in the dark, in the damp, in the mist rising and falling, hands aching, squeezing, over wet spray down weaving through air, cross breeze and current, in the dark, rising and falling gently, to a beach, aching, to a beach, squeezing, in the dark, holding, through mist rising and falling, to a beach, to a beach, to a beach . .
(*They fall on the beach.*)

ALL
(*The actors divide the lines among themselves.*)
In the dark.
On a beach.
Alone.
Aching.
In the mist.
In the dark.
On a beach.
Alone.
21. *They call each other.*
22. *They find each other. Pencroff strikes a match; the others move to him.*

ALL
(*The actors divide the lines among themselves.*)
We are alone.
We are alone on an island.
We have nothing.

And some are missing.
We are alone, and some are missing.
We are alone, and we have nothing.
We are alone on an island.

Event Eleven
GIFTS

After falling from the stage, Smith goes to one of the couple, Top to the other, one with a loaf of bread, one with a bottle of wine. After the match goes out, lights come up on the separated couple. The two actors present the wine and the bread to the couple and leave. All the actors leave. The couple may or may not share the bread and wine with the rest of the audience.

SUPPLEMENTARY MATERIAL

The following is the raw material of the flight in episode 12 of Event Ten. The actors draw from it, add to it, develop it, swap it. It is their flight and their consciousness of the flight, the storm and their experience of the storm.

HERBERT
I'm going to live longer than any.
I'm going to live
Longer than you.
Lucky to live,
To live forever.

If I could talk to a man a mile away,
If I could talk to a man I can't see,
I tell him and he tell me,
If I could reach my hands beyond my hands,
If I could stretch my arms beyond my arms,
Take the words, the words we say,
I the man, and the man me:
If we could talk to each other across the sea.

I'm going to live
Longer than any,
Longer than you
I'm going to live.

As I go running, wondering, here and there,
It's happening. It's happening.
Someone is doing it.
Right now.
It's bursting, it's exploding,
Somewhere I have never been,
Something I'm missing,
As I go running here and there:
He is putting it in his pocket.
He knows how.
It won't do. It can't do:
People said: It never did do.
But a man rose up and said, I'll do it.
He talked to a man over the land.
He is wiring the land:
He knows how.
From Washington to Baltimore,
He knows how.
From Baltimore to Boston,
Boston to Newfoundland,
Newfoundland to the sea,
Talking all the way to the edge of the sea,
Breathing on the land, to the edge of the sea,
To the Atlantic, marching to the sea,
Like a drummer, drumming to the sea,
A man on the land lying down
All the way to the sea:
He is there, he is there.
He knows how.
In one leap he is there.
He has broken the ground.
As I go running wondering, hot and staring,
He is putting the map in his pocket.
He is putting the land in his pocket.
Which is mine? Lord, which is mine?
I'm going to hustle.
It is gone. It is gone:
They are left behind.
He is wiring the land:

A man, a man,
A hammer and pickaxe man,
A man with his hands,
He is wiring the land,
Incredible dollars,
He is putting the map in his pocket.
Which is mine?
From Washington to Baltimore,
Baltimore to Boston,
Boston to Newfoundland,
Newfoundland to the sea,
Lying on the land all the way to the sea,
Like an army, conquering to the sea,
Like a boy, throwing stones in the sea,
Like a king, weeping by the sea.

If we could talk to each other,
If I could talk to you
And you could talk to me,
If we could talk to each other across the sea.
All in one time.
I'm going to live,
I'm going to live,
Longer than any.
Longer than you,
Lucky to live
To another day
To live to a time
A time to live:
Forever.

If I could talk to a man across the sea.
A man rose up and said: I'll do it.
I know how. I know how. It will do.
It can do. I can do. And he did.
Where is mine?
As I go running here and there,
He is reaching his arm beyond his arm,
He is stretching three miles to the bottom of the sea:
He touches the shells.

He is there, he is there.
If I could talk to a man,
A man, a pickaxe man.
A man with his hands,
Holding the shells,
As I go running, wondering here and there.
He is knowing, gladly knowing:
He is counting,
His hand is touching the shells.
He sees, he classifies,
He is putting his house in order.
I'm going to hustle.
He is digging, he is tunneling,
He is managing, he is acting,
He is knowing the land,
He is spinning his fingers away, away.
Three thousand miles,
Irresistible dollars,
He is binding the sea,
As I go running, wondering, hot and staring,
He is putting the map in his pocket.
Where is mine? Lord, where is mine?
I'm going to hustle.
I am going to hustle.
  SMITH
Five determined men, full hurricane.
Equinoctial storm: five days.
Ravaging: coasts, cities, bridges.
Equator to the thirty-fifth north
Diagonally to the fortieth south
Surpassing even catastrophes
Havana 25 October 1810
Guadalupe 26 July 1825
In this world, knowledge of thy truth.
Havana 25 October 1810
Guadalupe 26 July 1825.

Who dost promise that when two or three are gathered together in thy
name thou wilt grant their requests.

Five determined men.
A column of air, rising.
Pressing us upward.
Gas leaking.
To the other side of the lines:
I never count my dead.
When two or three are gathered together.
Equator to the thirty-fifth north
Cities, coasts, bridges
Surpassing even
Havana 25 October 1810
Guadalupe 26 July 1825.
In this world, knowledge of thy truth.

Column of air, pressing. Pressing our feet. Gas leaking. Direction unknown. Speed and altitude unknown. Time unknown. Latitude, longitude. Day or night. No sense of motion. Clouds moving, like ourselves.
Wisps moving past, passing. Us passing wisps moving. Our own motion.
Not rising. Moving past each other moving, in relation to each other,
passing. No sense of moving, but we are moving, slipping past them
passing us, wisps going by, not rising. As though not moving. Gas
escaping. Gas leaking.

Who hast given us grace at this time with one accord to make our com-
mon supplication unto thee.

To the other side of the lines:
I never count my dead.
Speed up and build well:
How many bridges, Captain?
Hundred and eighty-two, sir. A man can do it.
How many miles? The same, sir.
Hammer and pickaxe.
Forty days, over the land,
The work of his hands:
Columbus to Corinth,
Corinth to Huntsville,
Huntsville to Athens,
Tuscumbia, Grand Junction, Memphis, Charleston:
A man can do it.
Hundred and eighty-two bridges,

Hundred and eighty-two miles:
Who hast given us grace
At this time. Forty days, sir.
Chasms deep and wide.
How many miles? The same, the same.
When two or three are gathered together.
Hammer and pickaxe. Picks and axes.
Pioneer's tools, all we had:
With one accord.
Spades, axes, picks, and hammers:
We made what we needed.
How many miles? The same,
Always the same:
The work of his hands,
His own hands, over the land:
Five determined men:
Havana 25 October 1810
Guadalupe 26 July 1825
Nashville to Chattanooga,
Chattanooga, Tupelo,
Roswell and Shallow Ford:
In this world, knowledge of thy truth.

Fulfill now, O Lord, the desires and petitions of thy servants, as may be
most expedient for them.

    SPILLETT
I look, and looking, see:
               I see
        Man like a king, ascending his throne;
He is enthroned in the winds:
        Yes, he mounts the hurricane, the equinoctial storm.
He knows how, he knows how.
He saw the secrets, it was the work of his hands:
        The work of his hands, his own hands:
Nature gave over:
        Gave up her mystery
To the work of his hands
        And his all-seeing eyes:
Her secret fluids, her currents, her courses, winds
              and mysteries;

ESCAPE BY BALLOON

Power, knowledge, energy, science:
    He knows how, he knows how.
    He gives the names.
    He has a vision,
    He has a dream delirious:
Five determined men
            rising from Richmond
                    through darkness;

Five free men
        escaping the prisoners
                below

Not seeing
        not knowing
                not hearing

Not guarding
        not winning
                not going

Not understanding:
He has learned the names:
    He only gave the names:
Nature gave over:
    Her fluids and courses, winds, currents, mysteries:
Instant information:
    I write what I see
So that you may know:
    He has learned the names.
He dreams, he sees, he names, he knows:
    He rules in the name of the names.
Now, man, climb on your throne:
    Now, take your place:
        Man enthroned.
        Man like a king.
        Using the powers.
        Binding the earth.
He knows how: he sees,
He has a vision,
        he has a vision,
                a dream delirious:

Five determined men
>> rising through darkness
>>>> from Richmond;
Five free men
>> escaping the prisoners
>>>> the guardian prisoners
The prisoners below them
>> who did not know the names.

I look and looking, see. I write what I see, so that you, not seeing, may not live in darkness. Exact information: man ascending: nature gave over: power, knowledge, energy, science, electricity. The wires dispersing: eyes seeing: man ascending: you knowing: exact information: the work of his own hands: he saw the secrets: he is binding the sea: you knowing man ascending not living in darkness he saw the secrets he gave the names he knows how the work of his own hands:

He has learned the names: he rules:
He dreams, he sees, he names, he knows,
He rules in the name of the names he knows.

We will peel the skin off the earth and harvest her treasure:
We will spend the treasure to write the names:
We will write the names on the trees, for knowledge:
We will use the knowledge to reap the earth.

>> Exact information
>> Man like a king
>> Giving the news
>> Man like a god
>> Using the powers
>> Knowing how
>> Reaping the earth.

He has a vision,
>> he has a vision,
>>>> his dream delirious:
Five determined men
>> rising through darkness
>>>> from Richmond;
Five free men
>> escaping the prisoners
>>>> the guardian prisoners

The prisoners below them
        who did not see
                or know the names.

PENCROFF

What next? What next? I saw a man digging the earth. He is opening it up. He is mining. He is digging. He is working the earth. He peels it. He plows it. He strips it. He quarries it. He reaps it. He is touching its treasure. He is binding. He is taming. He is tunneling. He is dredging. He is building. He is laying the rails. He digs. He works. He drains. He cuts. He moves. He knows. He is tasting the harvest.

He knows how. Twelve times around the world: the women are saying their prayers.

I saw a chief in a homburg hat. I saw a fat queen. I saw a temple filled with cats. A ship five times bigger, five times bigger.

They said: it will not do. It cannot do. It's impossible it should do. Won't do. Can't do. Never could, never does, never did do. If it could have done, it would have done already.

I saw a man, sending words. Dot dot dot: all in one time. I saw a ship with six masts: five times bigger. Five funnels six masts two paddle wheels fifty-eight feet. I saw a coolie in a stovepipe hat. Twelve times around the world: wonders and marvels. All over the world, the women are saying their prayers. The sea is not hearing the sailors, no, the old men are tired, the children are bickering. And when they see us coming, well, then, they put on their hats. The paradise birds are stretched in a row. Not the best ones, of course. Oh, no. The best ones are gone. The next best, ten shillings each. I saw a king in a chintz suit. I saw a boy in a stovepipe hat. Only a boy, a Chinese boy, wearing a hat. And a frock coat: a coolie in a stovepipe hat. I saw a machine eating the earth.

Wherever we go, we are taking it with us. Five determined men: what we need, we make: he knows how, he knows how. Sometimes carpenter, sometimes smith, sometimes mason, sometimes chemist. Clothing and safety, hammer, trowel, pick, and axe: he knows how: the work of his own hands. Canals, mines, quarries, iron and cable, farm and housing, telegraph, machines, railroads, dams and electricity: the work of his hands, his own hands, and his all-seeing eyes. We will reap the earth. We will harvest her treasure. We will bind her. We will strip her. We will peel her skin. We will open her up. We will mine her. We will quarry her. We will flay her. We will work her. We will tame her. We will cut her down. We will plow her. We will dig her. We will tunnel her.

We will drain her. We will move her. We will work her. We will own her. We will reap her treasure. We will know her secrets. We will taste her harvest.

All over the world, the women are saying their prayers. The children are diving for pennies, the temples are filled with cats, the sea is not hearing the mariners, no. And when they see us coming, well: then they are putting on their hats.

I saw a ship, five times bigger, five times bigger: incredible dollars: five funnels, six masts two paddle wheels fifty-eight feet three thousand miles of wire: unbelievable tons: won't do, can't do, never could, never does, never did do. And when the signal reached New York, why, then, all the bells began to ring, and the guns were booming and the fireworks exploding and the sailors cheering and the queen was talking and the people listening: on earth peace, good will toward men.

I saw a chief in a derby hat. (Etc.)

NEB

In the storm, Lord, in the windy sea:
He's the One whose service makes you free.

Now the Lord said, Jonah, get up, go preach my people and pray:
He ran as fast as he could go the other way;
    Lord, Lord, in the windy sea:
    He's the One whose service makes you free.

And the Lord said, Jonah, it's the people of Ninevay,
But he took a ship and sailed away;
    Lord, Lord, in the windy sea:
    He's the One whose service makes you free.

So the Lord sent a wind out over the sea,
Said, Each man call out to his own idea of me;
    Lord, Lord, etc.

They looked for Jonah, he was sleeping and the crew
Said, Jonah, what on earth we going to do with you?
    Lord, Lord, etc.

And Jonah woke up in a temple or a jail,
Round him the bars or flying buttress of a whale;
    Lord, Lord, etc.

But the whale spit him up at the Lord's command,

110

ESCAPE BY BALLOON

Yes, it vomited out Jonah upon the dry land;
    Lord, Lord, etc.

He wrapped him in a blanket and began to preach the word:
He said, When my soul fainted I remembered the Lord;
    Lord, Lord, etc.

Now you people of Ninevay livin' too red, white and blue,
But your lying vanities going to come back on you,
    Lord, Lord, etc.

And you people, livin' too blue, white and red,
With your high-flying, gas-filled solo trips in the head,
    Lord, Lord, etc.

But I been down to the bottom of the hills,
Where the dark and deep closed in and the weed wrapped round my
skull;
    Lord, Lord, etc.

That's the upside-down land of first-shall-be-last,
Of more joy in Heaven for the slow than the fast,
    Lord, Lord, etc.

Where finder takes none and losers keep,
Where the slave shall be free and the winners weep:
    Lord, Lord, etc.

You folks better watch out, laying your track and your steel,
Because the machine's going to run you under its wheel,
    Lord, Lord, etc.

You'll be swallowed like Babylon, like Jonah in the tale,
In your high-flying upside-down air-swimming whale;
    Lord, Lord, in the windy sea:
    He's the One whose service makes you free.

Escape by Balloon by W.E.R. La Farge in collaboration
with the Firehouse Theater Company was performed in the
spring of 1972 at the Firehouse Theater, San Francisco.
It was directed by Sydney Walter. Music was composed
by John Franzen. The performers were Joe Blankenship,
Steve Bradley, Muniera Christensen, Robert Crutcher,

Michael Harrel, Birgitte Hotchkiss, Marlow Hotchkiss, and Antoinette Maher. (The role of Spillett was double cast in this production, being played alternately by Muniera Christensen and Marlow Hotchkiss.) Musicians were John Franzen and Nancy Walter.

ROBERT AULETTA

Stops

for Carol and Danny

STOPS

The lights come up on Mattie. She takes three steps, stops, looks at the audience, and smiles.

MATTIE

I'd offer you a fig newton, but I don't have any. I'm all out of 'em. (*She takes three steps, then stops.*)

In spite of what I once knew, I go to the house of friends. (*pause*)

Off in the distance, behind a great hedge. Secluded, comfortable. (*She takes three steps, then stops.*)

I have two friends. Nice ones. One like the other. And both like me.

(*calls off into the distance*) How close we've always been. How sensitive to each other's needs.

(*to the audience, lifting up her dress*) I'm covered with bruises. From head to toe. I fall down a lot.

(*calls off into the distance*) Don't I? Isn't that true?

(*to the audience*) I often have the need to verify. (*pause*)

Oh, I've always been clumsy. It's been my way. (*She takes three steps, then stops.*)

I have three friends. But one is dead. The two live ones are alive. They're nice. They're like me. The dead one is dead. He's like nothing you've ever seen. He's somewhat awful to remember. But I do. Often. On days like today. On days that contain some mystery. That's when I remember that dead one.

(*calls off into the distance*) Yoo hoo, yoo hoo.

(*to the audience*) They're hard of hearing, you know. And their hearing aids are badly out of date. (*pause*)

Hard to hear for them that lives over there. In the morning it's better. Sound carries better. Yes, in the morning I often believe that the sound of my voice just reaches them. Even when they've shut their hearing aids off. Even when they've shut their windows, and stuck their heads under their pillows. Even then, if I try hard, I can reach them. (*She stomps her foot.*)

Oh, I shouldn't do that.

(*calling off into the distance*) Did you prepare the hot water for my aching feet?

(*to the audience*) Of course they did. They're sweet dear ones. Like you. You're all sweet dear ones. Even you others who are bastards. You're sweet dear bastards. (*She smiles.*)

They're only words that I'm saying. So why not say anything? (*She smiles.*)

You know what I mean. And if you don't, you're dumb. (*She takes three steps, then stops.*)

Once I had three sweet dear bastards for friends. And on Sundays we would sup together. That is, if we could stand the ordeal. (*Pause, and she loses her balance for a moment.*)

Something is disordered. (*long pause*)

I stink the stink of a lousy stinking God. (*She smiles.*)

I didn't mean that. You'll vouch for that. I'm sure you'll vouch for that. (*She takes two steps, then stops.*)

Oh, how those lousy stinking bastards loved to sup at my table. I used to set a nice table. The nicest on the block. And used to set red flowers everywhere. Hillyhopes, or something of that sort, those red flowers were called. I'll bet they're still called that. Or something of that sort. Even to this day.

(*calls off into the distance*) Pluck some red flowers for me.

(*to the audience*) They won't. I bet they won't pluck even one. And I want bunches.

(*calls off into the distance*) I've told on you. I've squealed.

(*to the audience*) They are guilty of outrages of many sorts and assorted kinds. Each more heinous than the other. Just thought I'd let you know.

(*calls off into the distance*) I just let them know. And by God, are they furious.

(*looks at the audience*) You've never seen such a miserable bunch of furious bastards in your whole life. They're chewing on their lips. They're spitting blood.

(*smiles*) Don't worry. I've always been — how might you say it — on the brink, teeter-tottering. (*pause*)

Teeter-tottering on the brink, my mother used to say. And even if she never said it, it's what she meant to say. The flannel-faced bitch.

(*calls off into the distance, painfully*) Mother.

(*to the audience*) I only do that to make her think I care. (*pause*)

Poor thing, so dead. (*pause*)

She was born dead, my flannel-faced mother. And went through life in that exact same condition until one day the doctor finally made it legal. (*pause*)

Though we cried real tears. Or something closely approximating them. (*pause*)

What they were exactly, I'll probably never know. Or never really care to know. Though I am a bit curious to know if their chemistry was truly human or not. Is there a chemist . . (*She takes two steps, then stops.*)

(*calls off into the distance*) Mother.

(*to the audience*) I was going to make a joke about a chemist being in the house. (*pause*)

And if there is, bless his almighty soul.

(*calls off into the distance*) Mother, did you really drink iodine before meals, as we children used to say? That's what we thought made you so mean. It's only idle curiosity that impels me to ask you now, Mother. Idle curiosity that forces me back into a land so far away, so gone. Was it iodine, Mother? Or were all us children just dreaming? Tell me, Mother, were your beverages ordinary? And was it our dreams that were extraordinary?

(*to the audience*) Nothing of the kind. My mother drank turpentine. Gallons of it. The north woods variety, designed to kill horses. But with her it produced hardly a hiccup.

(*calls off into the distance*) Isn't that right, Mother? You were tough, but you were refined.

(*to the audience*) Her beverages were extraordinary. And our dreams were extraordinary. A monstrous brood, each and every one of us. Drunk on each other's vapors. (*pause*)

And to this day I still remember each and every one of us. Though it would have been grace to have forgotten it all. (*pause*)

We were a jolly family. Known in and around the neighborhood for our laughter. For it never stopped. Day in and day out. Even to this day we are remembered for it. (*pause*)

It's hard to kill a jolly family. In fact, it's goddamn near impossible. (*pause*)

Don't think they didn't try. Oh, they did. Oh, they really did. Droves of them. (*pause*)

There was always a frier in the fire. There was always a mat for the cat. And a pat on your head. And a kick in the ass to round out the day. (*She takes two steps, then stops.*)

In those days families were special. They had an aroma and fragrance so often missing from present-day reality. (*pause*)

It was the smell of their feet. (*pause*)

All the members wore filthy feet. And to show contempt for the other members, they very rarely changed their feet. And worse than that, they often took to exhibiting those feet under the noses of the other members. To reek havoc. To cause discomfort. Their motives were simple but powerful. (*pause*)

Dark deeds were done in the past. Dark days were lived in the past. (*pause*)

And may the past be damned. And those that congregated there, may they never know happiness. (*pause*)

Or light. Or television in the afternoon, when it's snowing outside, and your pension check has just arrived, and there's honey in the tea. (*She takes a few steps and falls down.*)

I keep falling down. I'm always falling down. Why am I always falling down? (*pause*)

Because I'm a dimwit. Because it's my nature. (*She tries to get up.*)

Piss on the high water, said Captain Bligh. And let the low water watch out for itself. (*She gets to her feet.*)

Another amazing man, that Captain. Though he's probably now dead like the rest of the crew. Under the sea. (*pause*)

Under the sea. (*She takes two steps, then stops.*)

We were a glorious brood. We all had faces like cats. We stuck together. We warmed each other. I remember many times in the early morning watching the snow fall against the window, listening to the brood purr. (*pause*)

Listening to the purring brood. (*pause*)

Listening to the roar of the purring brood. (*pause*)

Funny, but they always reminded newcomers of ravens. (*pause*)

Newcomers never stayed long among us. (*pause*)

We had our ways. And they were the right ways. And even if they weren't, what else could we do?

(*calling off into the distance*) Yoo hoo, yoo hoo. I'm coming round the mountain. I'm coming. (*pause*)

It is Mattie. It is I.

(*to the audience*) Is there a chemist on the premise?

(*smiles*) And if there is, bless his almighty chemistry set.

(*calling off into the distance*) It is Mattie. It is I. Do you not remember?

(*to the audience*) In those days I had a different name. It sounded similar to the one I use now. But it meant such different things. (*pause*)

Sometimes in the morning, when it is clear and still, and their hearing aids are working perfectly, I swear, they can hear me. They rise up in their beds and say: it is she! Coming to visit! She of the whitened hair! And then they lock their doors. And bolt them. And double lock them again. And then go back to bed. Pulling the woolen blankets around their ears. (*pause*)

The old have such difficult ways. But I don't mind. I easily adapt to circumstances. I fit right in. It's my way. (*She takes two steps, then stops.*) I was never a lover. Not in my heart, or in any other place. I guess you might say, it was a fault of character, some sort of awkward lack.

(*smiles*) Don't believe what I say. It's only words. They go their own way. (*pause*)

It's raining not far from here. On people whom I don't even know. (*pause*)

I was never a lover. But I consorted with lovers. First-rate lovers each and every one of them. They wore purple shirts and flowers. Their hair was shiny, their faces flushed, and the wine they drank was exceptionally rare. Mattie, they would say. Mattie, Mattie, they would always say. (*pause*)

It's a long way to Tipperary. But I think I would hate the place anyway. (*pause*)

It's where the Irish live.

(*calling off into the distance*) It is I. The child.

(*to the audience*) They make believe they don't hear me. They look the other way. (*pause*)

They make believe they don't fear me. They turn their fear the other way. (*pause*)

But I fear them, indeed I do. In retrospect, and in present-day reality. (*pause*)

Fear is part and parcel of all the Christmas parcels.

(*cries out*) Why don't they come for me? Why don't they carry me away? (*pause*)

Father did not cry real tears when Mum, or Mommy, or Mom, or Ma, or Mama, or Mother died. What Father cried was simpering music when Mum, or Mom, or Mama, or Mommy died. (*pause*)

One summer afternoon the sky was splayed by heat lightning. The brood was drunk about the streets. (*pause*)

And Father cried simpering music. From one room to the next. From morning till night till morning. (*pause*)

Out of tune. Squeaky. (*pause*)

I held a red coverlet around me. And underneath I was naked. (*pause*)

I was a demented young lady. (*pause*)

I stood on top of the tenement, and took the coverlet off. (*pause*)

From the top of the tenement one could see the tops of other tenements. (*pause*)

And on the top of each stood a naked young lady watching a red coverlet fall.

(*violently*) I was always a lover, but there was never anyone left to love. (*pause*)

The red coverlet fell two hundred feet. (*pause*)

Mother never knew what hit. Though we had been expecting the worst. Some of us praying against it. Some of us praying for it. (*pause*)

Nowadays it's hard to sort out who was doing what. (*pause*)

But one thing is sure, we always got the worst. Each and every one of us. It was our way (*pause*)

Father's underwear was shabby. (*pause*)

He worked by his instincts. But he was not an instinctive man. (*pause*)

He had little else to go on. (*pause*)

I offered no help. I was never of any assistance to any of them. (*pause*)

His shoes were even shabbier than his underwear. Though highly polished. Though strongly polished. You can always tell a man by his shoes, he said, each day of his life. (*pause*)

I believe that. Even to this day. When there is little else . . to grab onto. I still believe . .

(*violently*) Shoes is true! (*pause*)

I'm sure. (*pause*)

He wouldn't lie. (*pause*)

He wouldn't know how to lie. (*pause*)

He was a dull man. But with shoes of a high polish. And a straightforward manner. And a keen sense of expectation. That was admired by many. Though it didn't save him. (*pause*)

Nor did it I. (*She closes her eyes, then opens them.*)

(*calls off into the distance*) Father, Father, your shoes of a high polish, and your face so deathly pale. (*pause*)

Simper me some music. Simper me some of your sweet music. (*pause*)

My hand had always been smaller than most. But when it grabbed, it compensated for its lack of size by never letting go. (*She reaches out and grabs.*)

Next to my father's hand, my hand growing smaller each second. Next to my father's hand, my hand has almost disappeared. (*She withdraws her hand.*)

We did have our times, didn't we? Our ups and our downs. Our ins and our outs. Our dogs and our cats. Our pukes and our vomits. Our summers and our snows. (*pause*)

Though I never took much of it seriously. Always lighthearted about everything around me. Let it come. Let it go. What's the difference? (*pause*)

It was only life. They were only people. (*pause*)

They lived. And they died. And I follow their example. There's not much more to it. (*She takes two steps, then stops.*)

On to the house of friends. (*She takes two steps, then stops.*)

To the glorious house, of glorious friends. (*pause*)

A game of monopoly, a tickle of brandy, a laugh and a joke. (*the sound of thunder*)

Oh, dear. (*The lights begin to dim.*)

The brood always loved the rain. They moved easily in it. Sometimes they held newspapers over their heads. Sometimes nothing. Water sleeking their backs. Their shoes soggy. Mouths open. Hearts beating. (*pause*)

They loved it! Their hair hanging in strings and ringlets. Jumping across puddles. Howling across puddles. (*the sound of rain falling*)

Jumping into puddles. Howling into puddles. To their knees. To their thighs. To their throats. The sewers overflowing. (*thunder*)

The sewers gurgling. The brood gurgling. The sky gurgling. (*pause, then change of tone*)

I would lick the ice cream off his fingers. (*She takes two steps, then stops.*)

Equal in strength. Equal in speed. They would race. (*thunder*)

Like horses. They would race. (*pause*)

Like golden, like silver, like black. (*thunder*)

They would race to the house of friends. (*She takes two steps, then stops.*)

But one of the brood slipped, and hit his chin on the curb. His face running blood. (*pause*)

My blood! My blood! (*pause*)

And the rest of the brood laughed. Then the face running blood laughed. And rose up from the gutter, and began to race. A bloody, running, laughing face. It raced the brood down. And emerged the victor, emerged the strongest of the brood. Its name was Michael. (*pause*)

I would lick the ice cream . . (*pause*)

Its name was Michael. The face that of a saint. (*pause*)

Then they entered the radiant house of radiant friends. Music fastened to everything. To the red fire and the red walls. To the black chairs and the black sofa. To the round black table. To the food and the drink. To the beer and the wine and the whiskey. To the ham, and the rolls, and the sausage, and the pickles, and the smoked fish, and the long round loaves, and the fat round loaves, and the cold roast, and the cold chicken, and to the six different types of cheese, and to the soup, and to the salad, and to the ice cream, and to the coffee steaming clouds through the room, and to the pastries of assorted kinds, and to the chocolate nougat candies, and to the mints. (*pause*)

To the lovely after-dinner mints. (*pause*)

The music entered it all, like veins. (*pause*)

Oh, they all had such lovely hands. (*thunder*)

Which they wiped on their shirts, and pants, and jackets, and on the slipcovers, and on the draperies, and on the walls and the rugs, and on the lamps and on the floors, and all over the faces and the bodies and the clothes of the people sitting next to them, and even all over the people running away from them, the people running all over the house. (*pause*)

They were never known for their table manners. They were never loved for their decorum. (*pause*)

The people running all through the house. With the brood howling behind them. (*pause*)

122

They were often overenthusiastic. They often did not know when to stop. (*pause*)

And they left stains: pickle, salami, mustard, meat, chicken, chocolate stains, ice cream stains, coffee stains, blood stains, urine stains, semen stains everywhere. Everywhere! (*pause*)

Everything and everybody tottered around heavy with their stains. Reeling with their stains. Half crazy with their stains. Which never washed off. Which were like acid. Which ate through fabric and furniture and flesh alike. (*pause*)

Their presence was vividly felt in that radiant room. (*pause*)

They made their mark. They always made their mark. (*pause*)

But still they were loved, totally loved. (*pause*)

Each one of them had known total love. (*pause*)

The taste and the smell of it. The servitude of it. (*pause*)

Eternally.

(*calls off into the distance*) What was it like? What did it feel like?

(*to the audience*) I was never a lover, but neither have I ever denied anyone love. (*She takes two steps, then stops.*)

Never! (*pause*)

If there's a man alive that thinks that, let him step forward. Now! (*She looks around. She smiles. She takes two steps forward, then stops. She takes two more steps, then stops. It has stopped raining. The light is brighter. Jeff, an old man dressed in shabby clothes, enters behind Mattie. He coughs. Mattie hears him, but does not turn around.*)

Have you come to speak on my behalf? Is that why you have come, as a witness to my life? (*Jeff mutters.*)

Then I take it you know the truth.

(*to the audience*) He will tell you the truth of my life. (*Jeff mutters.*)

Come to me. Touch me. (*Jeff mutters angrily.*)

Come, come touch. You are my witness, aren't you? Thus you have the privilege of intimacy. (*Jeff mutters angrily.*)

Are you not a witness? Are you nothing? Are you a stray? (*She turns around.*)

I know you not.

    JEFF

I'm Jeff. (*She takes two steps toward him, then stops.*)

    MATTIE

I know no Jeff.

JEFF

Like Mutt and Jeff. Like the comic strip. (*She takes two steps toward him, then stops.*)

MATTIE

I know no comic strip.

JEFF

I wander about. (*She takes one step, then stops.*)

MATTIE

Touch me anyway. (*Jeff laughs.*) Don't do that! (*pause*)

JEFF

I've bought a new truss. (*He fiddles with his truss.*)

MATTIE

What?

JEFF

A new truss. At a sale at the surgical store.

MATTIE

Is it a great improvement?

JEFF

Huh?

MATTIE

Is it more comfortable, durable, lighter, more sanitary, does it give you greater freedom?

JEFF

It makes me happy.

MATTIE

Then it's all those things and more. Then it's a good truss.

JEFF

Huh?

MATTIE

Rejoice.

JEFF

I shouldn't wander about.

MATTIE

No.

JEFF

It's bad for me. I can get overexcited.

MATTIE

What?

JEFF

(*getting overexcited.*) I can get overexcited.

MATTIE

I think I heard you the first time.

JEFF

It's bad for me.

MATTIE

I can see why. (*pause*) Tell me what you know, Jeff?

JEFF

I know I shouldn't get overexcited.

MATTIE

Yes. Yes. If only I could have known that. That's truly something important. But what else do you know?

JEFF

I know how to make ends meet.

MATTIE

How does one do that?

JEFF

By cutting corners.

MATTIE

And how does one accomplish that?

JEFF

By doing without.

MATTIE

By doing without what? Exactly what, Jeff?

JEFF

By doing without whatever is not absolutely essential.

MATTIE

And what is the result of all this . . denial? (*Jeff laughs.*) Come now, tell me, in your own words.

JEFF

The result is . .

MATTIE

Spit it out.

JEFF

Happiness.

MATTIE

Complete happiness?

JEFF

Yes.

MATTIE

Has it worked for you? Have you attained . .

JEFF

I am completely happy.

MATTIE

(*calls off into the distance*) Why haven't I been told this before? (*pause; to Jeff*) It probably would not have worked for me.

JEFF

It works for everybody.

MATTIE

How do you know?

JEFF

I've seen it with my own eyes.

MATTIE

I hope you don't mind me saying this, Jeff, but you don't look completely happy to me. In fact, you look downright miserable.

JEFF

Inside I am a different man. (*He fiddles with his truss. It starts to get dark.*)

MATTIE

And your shoes are not highly polished. (*A siren is heard in the distance.*)

JEFF

Inside I'm altogether different. (*He exits.*)

MATTIE

You can always tell a man by his shoes. Or by his eyes, or by his hair, or by the words he does not speak. (*She resumes the direction she was going. She takes two steps, then stops. She takes two more steps, then stops.*) Oh, Michael, Michael, you never wore a truss. Ever. (*pause*)
His back against the window, the window against the light . . Mother would have had him for herself.
(*calls out*) Michael. (*pause*)
It's good you died so early. (*pause*)
Forgive and forget, I always say. Because it has forgotten you. (*She takes two steps, then stops.*)
But it does not let go. Even though the mind wills it. Even though the body pushes it away. (*A young man wearing a white uniform, and carry-*

126

ing a broom, enters. He begins to sweep up the stage. Mattie barely notices him. She addresses the audience.)
And look at you! You're so happy, so rested. So sweet, so sweet. *(pause)*
Once I was the happiest sweet person known. *(pause)*
But somehow . . yes, the brood turned against each other. Each one became a dog to the other. *(pause)*
They ran through the streets like a pack of dogs. *(pause)*
I am riddled with tooth marks. *(pause)*
I dropped the red coverlet. Then stood there watching the red coverlet drop. *(pause)*
I wanted to drop myself on the dropped red coverlet. *(pause)*
The brood howled as they ran down the wet streets. Their fur was soaked in blood and water, slobber and beer. They were running to their graves. All decked in holly and slobber. *(pause)*
Under a lamppost stood a skinny white bitch. The bitch was shivering. And she had a cut paw, which she held up. *(pause)*
The bitch licked her paw. *(pause)*
In other words, she licked her blood. *(pause)*
She liked it. *(The Young Man finishes sweeping, and exits.)*
(calls off into the distance) I am coming to thee. With my brush and comb. To fix your white hair. *(pause)*
The red coverlet lay like a heart-shaped drop of blood on the street. In those days there were horses. They reared up and cried out when they saw it. *(pause)*
I am toothed with riddle marks! *(pause)*
There were horses! *(The Young Man enters pushing a hospital bed. He places it stage right of the traffic light. Now he walks over to Mattie.)*
I stood like a statue on the rim of a building. Because I was a statue on the rim of a building. For I never was a human child. Nor did I ever live in a human land. *(He puts his arm around her, and begins to walk her slowly toward the bed.)*
Why was I not pushed? The coverlet lay waiting for me. And I stood above it, about to, about to . . But I was not pushed! *(pause)*
I was saved. By an angel. *(They reach the bed. The Young Man helps Mattie to sit on it.)*
I wish I could find that angel now. I would speak to him heart to heart, then spit blood and ash into his face. *(The Young Man takes off her shoes, then unbuttons her dress at the throat. Now he helps her get under the covers.)*

127

(*calls off into the distance*) I will only be a moment, just a sweet moment. (*to the Young Man*) They are the last of the last, the ones who will speak on my behalf. (*He begins tucking her covers in.*)
They are probably speaking now, about my life, about the beauty of my life. Listen. It sounds like bees.

YOUNG MAN

Yes, just like them, just like a swarm of bees. (*She grabs his hand, and licks his fingers.*)

MATTIE

Vanilla. (*He smiles and exits.*)
To lie in a red room, to sleep content in a room made glowing red by love . . (*Suddenly she sits upright. Her face filled with terror.*)
Get out of here! Out! Out into the streets! (*pause*)
Please. (*She sinks back into the bed.*)
I'm still in charge. (*pause*)
I once had a husband. (*pause*)
I was interested in his betterment. (*pause*)
He did not understand my concept of betterment. (*pause*)
I tried very hard to clarify. (*pause*)
Still he fell behind in all my expectations. (*pause*)
And this brought much shame to him. (*pause*)
Much shame.
(*to the audience*) I showed them the human heart. And do you know what they did with it? They ate it! (*pause*)
My human heart! (*pause*)
There are things of great beauty in this world that people should not be allowed to touch. (*pause*)
Let alone eat.
(*calls off into the distance*) And you have witnessed it! The devouring of the human heart. Come and kneel down, and confess what you've seen. (*pause*)
They hear me, but they dare not come. (*pause*)
I moved like a saint among them, among all of them. Even those that hated me. (*Irene enters.*)
Don't come near me. (*Irene takes a few steps toward her.*)
Out! Out into the streets! (*Irene takes a few more steps.*)
You are not my witness. You are nothing to me. (*Irene rushes to her,*

128

and tries to embrace her. Mattie strikes her. Irene jumps back.)
Nothing. Nothing. (*Irene rushes out.*)
I am consumed. (*She closes her eyes.*)
There were horses. And the street was swift with them. And the sky, and the sky . . (*She opens her eyes. She gets out of bed.*)
The frost, the frost . . (*pause*)
I scratched it with my fingers from the inside of the window, and looked out as they took Mother's body away. (*She takes two steps, then stops.*)
I've seen the whole bastard thing with my eyes wide open. And I never flinched, or closed my eyes. I gritted my teeth, and stared the bastard thing right in the face. (*She takes two steps, then stops.*)
And it stared back, believe me. (*pause*)
I am riddled with tooth marks, from breast, to belly, to thigh. (*She takes two steps, then stops.*)
But I have wept for them. I have wept my heart's blood for all of them. Even for the worst of them. (*She takes two steps, then stops.*)
To their graves I have gone. In the cool air, in the cool air . . By the river, by the river . . (*pause*)
The last of the living. (*She takes two steps, then stops.*)
In those days there were horses. And they wore bells about their necks. Mother's body followed behind the clomp of horses, the sound of bells. (*She takes two steps, then stops.*)
And I danced for them! And I danced for them! As I do now. (*She begins to dance, while making the sound of bells. She does well, growing stronger and stronger; then suddenly collapses.*)
Why not drop a hook down, and swing it into me? Why not hoist me off, and dump me into the sea? (*She pulls herself along the ground.*)
Once I had a husband, and together we brought forth creatures. This is a registered fact. (*She pulls herself along the ground.*)
Drop your hook into me! (*She pulls herself along the ground.*)
You witnesses. You false witnesses. You are not there. You are dead. (*She pulls herself along the ground.*)
Once I had a friend, but now he is dead. But, oh, when he was alive . . Oh, you should have seen him then. (*She pulls herself along the ground.*)
When my husband was away at the store, among the crates, and the jars, and the cheese . . (*pause*)
I got nothing out of it. Nothing at all. I was trod upon. (*pause*)
Many times. (*pause*)

129

Always asking for more. (*She pulls herself along the ground.*)
All decked in holly and slobber. (*She lies there quite still. After a few moments the Young Man enters. He goes to her and picks her up. He carries her to the bed, and places her under the covers. Now he takes a strap from the bed, and secures her tightly. He exits.*)
(*to the audience*) Tell me about your life. Tell me all about it. (*pause*)
Don't be shy or afraid. Tell me about your beautiful past. Speak it to me. (*pause*)
About your first feelings and impulses. About how strong and fine they were. How pure. And high-grade. And about how those around you responded. About the gestures. About the faces. What did the faces resemble? And about the hands. What did the hands feel like? And about the hearts. Could you feel their hearts beating beneath their chests? And about the colors. What were the colors like? The colors of the rugs, the walls, the stairs, the sinks, the closets. Tell me all about the colors. And the smells. The smell of the snow. The wonderful smell of the snow. And the sky. The look of it. Tell me. Did it frighten you? And the funny faces you made. Make some of those funny faces now. Don't be afraid. Yes, that's beautiful. Those funny faces you're making are beautiful. And the darkness. Tell me about the darkness. The depth and the intensity of it. Its feel. The grit of it. Of what you lost in it. The black of it. If you died in it. Or if you lived in it. Tell me about it. Speak it to me. Speak the hatred of it to me. Don't be afraid. Spit it on me. Don't hold back. Spit it. That's why I am here. Spit. (*pause*)
That's good. That's fine. All together. Now we're one together. By the sea for a picnic. In the woods for a romp. Our pretty dresses. Our colored shirts. Sipping cider. Our heads thrown back. Our hair flying. The trees, the sky, the sea, our eyes. (*The traffic light goes out.*)
I'm glad, I'm glad. As you are. As we all are. As we all are glad. As we all are one. As we are together. (*pause*)
Her radiant white hair soft as an animal on the pillow. Her dead eyes . .
(*a crashing metallic sound*)

THE END

Stops by Robert Auletta was presented on February 1–5, 1972, at the Yale Repertory Theatre, New Haven, Connecticut. It was directed by Michael Posnick.

Cast of Characters

MATTIE	Joan Pape
JEFF	Jeremy Geidt
YOUNG MAN	Bill Gearhart
IRENE	Sarah Albertson

HAL LYNCH

3 Miles to Poley

Cast of Characters

MAMA
PAPA
HAL
HOBE

Time: Now and the past

3 MILES TO POLEY

ACT ONE

While the houselights are up we hear the quiet strumming of a guitar.
Then a man's voice gently sings "Rattlesnake":

Rattlesnake

Rattlesnake, oh, rattlesnake,
    What makes your teeth so white?
I been living in the bottom all my life,
    And I ain't done nothing but bite, bite,
Ain't done nothing but bite.

Muskrat, oh, muskrat,
    What makes you smell so bad,
I been living in the bottom all of my life,
    I'm mortified in my head,
I'm mortified in my head.

Groundhog, oh, groundhog,
    What makes your back so brown,
It's a wonder that I don't smotherfy,
    Living down in the ground,
Living down in the ground.

Rooster, oh, rooster,
    What makes your claws so hard,

Been a-scratching the gravel all of my life,
   It's a wonder I ain't tired,
It's a wonder I ain't tired.

Bluejay, oh, bluejay,
   What makes you fly so high,
Been a-robbing your cornfield all of my life,
   It's a wonder I don't die,
It's a wonder I don't die.

Slowly the houselights go to black. The song continues as the stagelights come up just enough to silhouette the objects onstage. As the song fades, the figure of a man enters, opens and walks through a screen door, and lets it slam with that remembered sound. He walks down to a table, strikes a wooden match, and "lights" an oil lamp (electrified). The general lights come up revealing a large stage strewn with set pieces. The set generally consists of two areas. One is a front porch. The other, in which the man is standing, is a kitchen. No attempt at realism need be made, for this is a memory play. The time and place is rural Alabama in the 1930s. If there is a sense of age about the properties it should be the age of use not disuse. Most of the set is in place but a few pieces have yet to be put in their ultimate positions. The porch consists of a raised platform with a screen door upstage. A shelf is on one end and there is a provision for a roof support. The porch is bare except for a rusty bucket with a wilted plant. An old broom stands by the door. On the shelf is a bucket of water with a gourd dipper, a blue enamel pan, and a rag towel. A gunnysack is tossed carelessly over an upstage corner. On the steps are a palmetto fan, a jackknife, a piece of wood, and a few shavings. In the "yard" there is an overturned rocker. In the kitchen there is a pine table covered with oilcloth, an old oil lamp (electrified), some scattered dishes, pans, and cutlery. The two chairs are rickety with rope seats. One of the chairs is upturned on the table. A wood stove is in the background near a screen door. A cupboard table with a faded skirt sits to one side. On the table is a bucket with a dipper, an enamel pan, a few odds and ends of dishes, a folded canvas apron, a half-pint mason jar, a pitcher, and an old "Philco"-type radio with a loosely hung aerial wire extending into the flies. An ancient guitar, elaborately inlaid with mother-of-pearl, leans against the cupboard. A small tin can is on the floor. A pair of worn shoes and socks are under the table. As the man "adjusts" the wick of the lamp, the stagelights get

brighter. The man is amusedly aware of this and adjusts the lamp an ex-
tra time or two and the stagelights dip accordingly. The man's manner is
open and friendly. When he speaks he has a soft southern accent. His
dress is casual, perhaps jeans and an open shirt.

MAN

These old lamps give just the right amount of light, don't they? (*He*
smiles at the audience and gives them a chance to smile back.) Hi-di. (*He*
moves upstage and carelessly tosses the matchbox on the warming shelf
of the stove. Turning back to the audience) My name is Hal Ryan. (*He*
waits a moment for a hint of recognition. There is none. Smiling, he
moves back to take the chair from the table.) You don't have to remember that but them of you that do will be better able to tell what's happening to who later on in the evening.

WOMAN

(*offstage*) Harol'? Harol'! Harol'! (*The voice is calling someone, not a*
lyrical remembered sound. Hal pauses and listens a moment, then rue-
fully he moves downstage.) · ·

HAL

Well, actually, my name is Harold Ryan. And that voice you just heard
correcting me is the voice of someone I used to know. And if my memory
holds out, tonight we're gonna talk to and with and about a lot of people
I used to know, because, well, that's why we're here.

As you can see I've gathered together a bunch of odds and ends, some
of them a little out of date, and we've arranged them in a certain way
so that with a little imagination they represent places I used to live. (*Hal*
moves to the porch, picks up a post, inspects it, and inserts it into the
platform in such a way that it stands upright. He looks up into the flies.)
See? With a little imagination you can almost see a porch roof. (*He*
moves into the "yard" again toward the overturned rocker.) We did all
this to help me remember and maybe it'll help you remember, too.
Memory is a tricky thing. (*He picks up the rocker.*) They say our sense
of smell brings back the sharpest memories. (*He sniffs the back of the*
chair. Nothing.) Just an old chair. (*He carries the chair up on the porch.*)
But things can make us remember. Sometimes it's something seen out
of the corner of our eye . . (*He has set the chair on the porch and in-*
advertently rocks it.)

MAN

(*offstage*) Dammit to hell! You worse'n your ma . . ! (*Hal turns quickly and stops the motion of the chair. The voice stops. Hal glances into the flies, then back to the audience.*)

HAL

Now there's the problem with memories. You don't always get what you want. You ever start out remembering that wonderful trip you took that time and wind up remembering how you forgot to tell the milkman and came home to a yard full of sour milk? Well, I have to be just as careful because there are a lot of things I want to tell you about . . (*picks up the bucket with the plant and moves it to a downstage corner of the porch*) but they're all mixed up with a lot of things I don't know how to tell you about. But I think I want you to know it all. (*He smells the foliage of the plant.*)

WOMAN

(*offstage*) Harol', come out from under there and water your granny's hydrangea . . (*Hal looks at the plant in mild surprise and puts it down.*)

HAL

See what I mean? (*He surveys the stage, finds everything is right, then moves to the porch steps and sits. He idly fans himself with the palmetto fan as he talks to the audience.*) So, our text tonight is the past. The "good old days." The good old days when I was a kid during the depression in my hometown of Opp, Alabama. That's right. Opp. O-P-P. For them of you that are a little vague on Alabama geography, from Opp it ain't but three miles to Poley. 'Course, that's just an old joke around Opp, but present looks deceiving, Poley used to be the sawmill capital of south Alabama . .

WOMAN

(*offstage*) You want to be a rent farmer? (*Hal stares at the fan, then puts it down. He picks up the knife and piece of wood gingerly, waits a beat to see if there will be a vocal reaction from the voices. There is none. He idly whittles as he continues.*)

HAL

But I didn't get you all here to talk about the town. I got you here to talk about the people. 'Course there was my family, that is the ones that lived there in the same house. There was me and my mama and my granddaddy, we all called him Papa, and my grandmamma and Uncle Edlo Edgar and Uncle Hub and Uncle Dan Daniel and Uncle Ernest and Uncle Joe Josephus and Aunt Anna Susanna and Aunt Bessie May and Aunt Rosey Lee and Aunt Rossy May . .

138

WOMAN

(*offstage*) You want to be a rent farmer? A rent farmer?

HAL

(*to the unseen voice*) Now, come on! (*He moves away from the porch.*)
I ought to say this too, I reckon. We were rent farmers. What we nowadays refer to romantically as sharecroppers. So I guess you never heard
of any of the family. But there are a lot of well-known people from Opp.
There's Vern Wilkerson; got his picture in the paper last year when he
made the fifteen-hundred-dollar club selling insurance down in Mobile.
Ralph Benton? He's got the Rooster Snuff concession for the whole state.
Cleb Buckalew; biggest worm man in south Alabama. And Erso Mor-
row. We're mighty proud of Erso. She has won second place in the National Truck Drivers' Rodeo up in Oregon two years in a row. That
Erso, she's as manly a woman as you'd ever want to meet.

WOMAN

(*offstage*) And all I've done! It's like I don't even belong!

MAN

(*offstage*) Dammit to hell, you worse'n your ma . .

WOMAN

(*offstage*) Don't bring Mama in this! You treated me . .

HAL

(*loudly*) All right, all right! (*back to audience*) You see? No matter how
hard you try to stay with one memory there's always another one trying
to crowd in. (*He ponders a moment, makes a decision and continues.*)
How do you remember yourself when you were little? In your memory
are you a tiny little person or are you the same size and other people
are bigger? That's the way it is with me. (*He kneels by the porch.*) Take
this porch. When I was about three or four years old I used to spend my
whole day underneath a porch like this. I don't think I even want to
get under there now but if I remember really hard . . I'm under the
porch. (*He rises and moves over near the cupboard.*) Now under the
porch don't seem like a great place to be but that's where I had to go
because that's where the doodle-bugs lived. A doodle-bug is a little gray
bug that eats ants and like I said, when I was three or four years old . .
(*He spots the mason jar on the cupboard. He chuckles, picks it up, ex-
amines it, and puts it back down during the following.*) When I was
three or four years old, having a jar full of doodle-bugs was my life's work.
And like all good things for kids to do there was a little chant that went
with catching doodle-bugs. And I have taken the liberty of making a

little song out of the little chant. (*He picks up the guitar and sits on the corner of the cupboard which is almost center. Sings*)

Doodle-bug, doodle-bug, come out of your hole,
    Your house is burned down and your babies are cold.

There's a doodle-bug living under my house,
    He don't make a sound, he's quiet as a mouse,
But he sees everything I do,
    He won't tell on me but he'll tell on you.

Doodle-bug, doodle-bug, come out of your hole,
    Your house is burned down and your babies are cold.

(*As Hal sings the stagelights change leaving him in a spot. The sounds of crickets, frogs, and whippoorwills swell up. The porch is bathed in the golden light of a summer's evening, the light softening everything it touches. At the end of the verse the screen door opens and Kate steps out onto the porch. Her age is 23–25. Her dress is a fresh print, puffed at the sleeves, not quite new but obviously not home-made. It is starched and ironed and very clean. It is the end of a hot day and she sits on the steps and fans herself with her fan. An occasional mosquito finds her and she slaps it casually but firmly. Her hands are seldom still; it is not frenzy but the reflex of years of work. After the song ends, Hal chants softly, intently.*)

Doodle-bug, doodle-bug, come out of your hole,
    Your house is burned down, your babies are cold.

(*Kate glances toward the space under the porch.*)

KATE

Come out from under there, honey, and sit with mama. (*Hal continues chanting.*) I declare it was hot today. It's good to get cleaned up and out of that hot kitchen. (*She looks at the shrunken potted plant.*) Look at Mama's hydrangea. Plumb wilted. Harol', come out from under there and water your granny's hydrangea. Come on, sugar. (*The screen door opens and Papa steps out onto the porch. He is a man in his sixties but he has enormous strength and vitality when he wishes to use it. He is dressed in a blue work shirt buttoned at the throat and wrists and a pair of bib overalls. Heavy brogans are on his feet but no socks. His clothes are as dirty and worn as Kate's are clean and bright. As he steps outside he carefully puts on a ragged flat-brimmed straw hat. Two keys to this man's character: He is vain about his looks in a hat and always wears it straight on his head; he is a storyteller in the best tradition. Papa glances at Kate, then checks the weather as he selects a straw from the broom which he uses as a toothpick. Finally he speaks.)*

PAPA

Hey, sister. (*Note: In this part of the country, "hey" is used as a greeting much like "hello" and has about the same emphasis. Kate ignores the greeting. Papa pauses, picking and sucking his false teeth.*) How come you left the table? (*No response.*) That summer squirrel et right good.

KATE

I didn't want any, Papa. It ain't good for you to eat squirrels this time of year. They got worms.

PAPA

Yeah, I hearn that, but I get tired of greens. A man's gotta have some meat now and again. (*Papa becomes aware of Hal's voice, chanting.*) Where you at you little 'scannel (*scoundrel*)? I hear you! (*He sits heavily in the rocker, bends over, and squints through a hole in the porch floor.*) I see you, you little rascal! (*He wiggles his finger in the hole as though he can see a child under the porch. When he sits back to relax we see that his hands move constantly also.*)

KATE

Harol', come out from under that house! Come on, leave them old doodle-bugs alone.

PAPA

Sister, let the boy be.

KATE

Papa, he don't need no more doodle-bugs! Harol'! Come out of there!

HAL

Yes'm. (*Carrying the mason jar Hal walks into the scene. This is a memory and Hal walks through the scene as an adult. Occasionally he reacts directly with the other actors but generally he is observing like the audience. He makes no attempt to "be" a child.*)

KATE

Oh, just look at you! You're as dirty as you can be!

HAL

Look what I got, Mama!

KATE

Another jar full of doodle-bugs! That's nice, honey. You want mama to keep them for you?

HAL

No'm, you lost my other ones! Papa, you want to see my doodle-bugs?

PAPA

Yes, shug, come up here and let me see them doodle-bugs. (*Hal moves up on the porch and squats beside Papa.*)

KATE

Papa, don't make over them bugs . .

PAPA

Let me see them bugs. Look at 'em wiggle! You ain't nothing but a doodle-bug yourself.

HAL

Papa, can I sleep with them tonight?

KATE

Yes, you can! And you can sleep with Papa, too!

PAPA

You sleep with them, they'll die.

HAL

Can we have a funeral?

PAPA

Yeah.

HAL

Can we sing "Aunt Rhody"?

PAPA

Yeah.

HAL

Daddy's dead.

KATE

Oh, Harol'!

HAL

Mama, did we sing "Aunt Rhody"?

KATE

Harol' . .

PAPA

Kate, he's just a baby.

KATE

Now, Papa, don't you tell me. I know he's a baby and I know his daddy's dead.

HAL

Papa, can we put them in a box and bury them?

PAPA

We'll get everybody together and have a funeral in the sass-garden.

KATE

Humph!

PAPA

Look at that one climbing up the glass. He's a big one, ain't he?

KATE

You'll go to anybody's funeral as long as it's in the sass-garden!

PAPA

What's ailing you?

KATE

Nothing!

HAL

Mama, Papa said doodle-bugs eat ants. Would they eat Aunt Rossy May?

PAPA

No, shug, little ants. Ants on the ground. Kate, we done the best we could. We always do the best we can.

KATE

Well, that sure wasn't much. I've tried to laugh it off but I guess you'all didn't even care.

PAPA

Now, dammit!

HAL

(*sings*)

> Go tell Aunt Rhody, Go tell Aunt Rhody,
> Go tell Aunt Rhody, the old gray goose is dead.

(*After the first line of the song, Papa joins in, relieved to change the subject but Kate has no intention of changing the subject.*)

KATE

Don't you dammit me! This family ain't never been much but we always helped our own. Always. I'm the oldest girl . .

PAPA

You always been treated as good as anybody . .

KATE

No! It's been three months since Mr. Ryan died up there in Birmingham and there ain't been a day passed that I ain't wondered why not one of you come to help. What could I do? Mr. Ryan never told me nothing about business. They just come and took the store. Said it was owed. All I got out of it was some little old screwdrivers and his watch. Nothing but his watch! I couldn't even send him home to be buried. Not one of you come up and helped me! Not one! And all I've done! It's like I don't even belong!

PAPA

Dammit to hell, you worse'n your ma . .

KATE

Don't bring Mama in this! You treated me just like you do her! That's why I let his people take his body. My husband is buried in Atmore! I couldn't even go to Atmore to his funeral! The last time this baby seen his daddy it was four o'clock in the morning at the funeral parlor in Birmingham before his people took his poor body to Atmore! You know how much Mr. Ryan hated Atmore! Why couldn't some of you come to help me? I wired you . . (*Kate has finally dissolved in bitter tears. Papa hands the jar back to Hal.*)

PAPA

Here, shug. Hush, Kate. (*Papa stands, moves down to the steps, and sits.*) Harol', fetch me the pan. Fetch me some water in it. Make haste. (*Hal goes to the shelf and dips water from the bucket into the pan. Papa begins rolling up his pants and untying his shoes. Hal brings the pan and puts it between Papa's feet, then goes to the corner of the porch, and stands. Everyone is helpless for a moment.*)

KATE

Papa, some of that I didn't mean. I know you got nothing here and you took us back. I guess I ought to thank God you was somewhere but every now and then I get to feeling so sorry about it all I just can't help myself.

PAPA

Shug, help Papa with his shoes. (*Hal kneels and removes Papa's shoes.*) Them feet's as black as a nigger's, ain't they? (*Hal sits at Papa's feet.*) That bottom land is rich. How many bales you reckon it'll make?

HAL

Papa? (*Kate's anger is spent.*)

KATE

It don't look too rich to me.

HAL

Papa?

KATE

I bet you'll be lucky to get half a bale a acre.

HAL

Papa?

PAPA

Yeah.

HAL

Can I wash my feet with you?

PAPA

In a minute.

HAL

My feet's as black as a nigger's, too.

PAPA

(*chuckling*) They is?

KATE

Harol', hush! Where you learning to talk like that?

HAL

Papa said his feet was black as a nigger's . .

PAPA

That's right, shug.

KATE

Now, Papa! Harol', nigger ain't a nice word!

HAL

But Papa said . .

KATE

Harol'! (*Hal sits, confused and subdued. Finally he speaks.*)

HAL

Papa, can I wash my feet with you? (*Papa starts to say yes but a decision has been forming in his mind. He takes his pocketknife from his pocket and hands it to Hal.*)

PAPA

Here, hon, play with Papa's knife. Don't you open it. (*Hal takes the knife and turns away delightedly. During the following his back is to the audience and he sits quietly. Papa steals a look at Kate and fidgets. He is caught on the horns of a confession that is an entertaining story. He is alternately contrite and expansive.*) Kate, I told them not to tell you 'cause I was ashamed. Didn't nobody not want to help. We all wanted to help. As soon as we got your wire we all said, "We got to help Kate!" You don't know this but ever'body in the family give me all the money they had. Rossy May didn't have but sixteen cents but she give it to me. You the only one of us that ever went to Birmingham. I didn't know what to do. We ain't got no automobile. I knowed I couldn't go in the wagon.

So, I went to Dan Richberg and asked him to take me in his taxi. Well, you know Dan hadn't never been to Birmingham neither but he said we'd go. For twenty dollars.

Sister, we didn't have no idea it was more'n two hundred mile and most of that cotton patch. We didn't hit but one strip of smooth road and that was in . . uh . . Montgomery. Dan was somewhat upsot. More than twenty dollars' worth of pieces fell off'n his taxi. We got stuck crossing a creek up near Brantley and I thought old Dan was gonna cry when his back seat washed out. I reckon what upsot him the most wasn't the seat but you know he had four gallons of whiskey and I seen it! (*The mention of illegal whiskey shocks Kate.*)

KATE

Papa! Don't shame me more!

PAPA

Now, Kate, I swear I didn't drink none of that whiskey. Even when we got lost and Dan wanted to drink, I wouldn't let him. No, sir! We fotched up in Birmingham cold sober. I never seen so many people in my life! There was more people on one street than I ever saw on fair day in Troy. And automobiles! Like fleas on a dog!

Kate, we drove up and down for two days! You know, they got lights on them streets to tell you which way to go? Dan couldn't get it through his head which color to go ahead on. Ever' po-lice in Birmingham musta stopped us. Ever' time one would we'd have to take off our coats and cover up that whiskey. One of them times I lost my vest. You remember my vest? Your mama was upsot about that vest! (*Something rings true and Kate is beginning to believe, incredulously.*)

KATE

If you was in Birmingham, why, my address was in the wire and the funeral home, too. Why didn't you come to the house?

PAPA

I didn't take the wire with me. You know I can't read so I didn't think about it. I figured I could just ask somebody on the street. (*accusingly*) Didn't nobody there know neither one of you!

KATE

God help this family! Just ask somebody on the street? You know how big Birmingham is? Why didn't you look in the phone book? (*Papa doesn't comprehend this at all.*)

PAPA

The what?

KATE

If you seen so many po-lices, why didn't you ask one of them?

PAPA

I never did like messing around with no po-lices. Besides, we had all that whiskey.

KATE

I was right there on Dale Street in Five Points waiting to hear from some of you. I never heard a word.

PAPA

Well, we'd a-stayed longer but Dan had to get back to Opp. Besides I didn't have but forty-three dollars when I started out and I spent ever' penny of that. (*He starts to figure on his fingers.*) There was twenty dollars to Dan . . (*The effort is too much. He looks to Kate for sympathy.*) We didn't have a bite to eat all the way home.

KATE

Good!

PAPA

Hadn't-a been for that whiskey . . uh . . shug! Hand Papa that rag. (*Hal reaches to the shelf and hands Papa the rag which he uses to dry his feet.*)

KATE

You don't have to hush. When you said whiskey I knowed you drunk it. It don't matter.

PAPA

Well, I finally told you. I'm 'shamed I didn't know enough to find you. None of us *never* just paid you no mind! (*The night sounds have been fading up and now we hear a chorus of frogs. The lights on the porch have faded to dusk.*) Shug, listen to them old bullfrogs. Let's me and you go get us a mess. (*Hal moves excitedly to get the gunnysack.*)

HAL

Papa, when you cut the legs off a bullfrog does the rest of the frog die? (*Papa answers absently while putting on his shoes.*)

PAPA

Yeah, I reckon so, hon.

HAL

Can we make some little boxes and bury them?

147

PAPA

Kate, this boy is gonna be a undertaker! No, shug, Papa was just a-funning. Them old frogs grow new legs just like a tadpole. Remember how your tadpoles growed new legs?

HAL

Uh-huh. Papa, my tadpoles died.

PAPA

Hush, Harol'. Come on, we gotta sneak up on them. (*Papa takes the gunnysack and he and Hal go off single file into the dusk. Hal stops upstage by the porch. Papa's voice drifts back as from a great distance, singing "Aunt Rhody." Kate listens as the singing fades under the night sounds.*)

KATE

I oughta be thankful but I can't be. I'm back in Opp! (*She rises and takes the pan and rag from the step. She carefully pours the water into the potted plant. Hal has turned to watch her. During the following he moves down to his original place by the cupboard. He picks up the guitar and picks softly under Kate's words.*) How'm I ever gonna get outta Opp. It don't even sound right. Opp! Well, he did try, I guess. It's a wonder he didn't get killed hisself. I bet him and Dan Richberg was drunk from the minute they left. (*She calls through the screen door.*) Mama! Mama, you better leave the flour out. They gone to get some frogs.

HAL

(*sings*)

> Down on my knees with a straw in my hand,
>   Calling that doodle-bug to beat the band,
> I want him to tell me all that's new,
>   Not about me but all about you.
>
> Doodle-bug, doodle-bug, come out of your hole,
>   Your house is burned down and your babies are cold.

(*As Hal sings, Kate wipes the pan and puts it on the shelf and spreads the rag to dry. She sits in the chair for a moment, resigned and trapped, staring out from the porch. The fading light makes a halo about her. At the end of the verse Kate stands, sighs, and goes inside. The chair rocks gently. For Hal, it is as though what has happened was just a single thought in his mind. He is aware the audience has shared the thought; it is one of the things he didn't know how to tell about. The song ends and still picking the guitar softly Hal moves over to the porch and rocks the chair. In the silence he looks cautiously up into the flies. Nothing happens. He puts the guitar on the rocker, moves up on the porch, and gets the broom. He looks out at the audience for a moment, then smiling he moves down the steps and sweeps the shavings into a neat pile. During the following he will ready a few things onstage, take the broom over to the kitchen set, retrieve his knife and piece of wood, etc.)* Me and a kid named Tyrone Price used to catch doodle-bugs all the time. I liked to catch them and keep them but Tyrone liked to catch them and step on them. You see, Tyrone had this gland problem. We was the same age but when I weighed forty pounds, Tyrone already weighed a hundred and forty and by the time I weighed a hundred and forty, there wasn't a scale in Opp big enough to weigh him. Me and Tyrone was lifelong friends but he begun to get the feeling very early that I was doing him wrong. When we was about five.

I remember I went over to Tyrone's house one day and there was Mrs. Price sitting on the back steps fanning herself and there was Tyrone on the porch standing on a Buffalo Rock Ginger Ale box up to the ironing board pushing a big old flatiron over a pair of overalls. I said, "Hey, Tyrone." Tyrone said, "Hey, Harol'." I said, "What you doing that for?" And Mrs. Price said, "I'm learning my boy to be a gentleman." Well, I wasn't but five years old so I didn't know what to say to that but just about that time them overalls caught on fire and Tyrone fell over backwards off the Buffalo Rock Ginger Ale box and he kicked over the ironing board and the flatiron fell on Mrs. Price's foot and she jumped up and slapped Tyrone and Tyrone begun to cry and I begun to laugh. And Tyrone said, "Harol', I'm gonna git you!" And the first chance he got he throwed me down and he set on me.

Well, I commenced to yell and squall so Tyrone slid up till he was sitting on my head. You ever have anybody sit on your head? That come to be the way Tyrone Price had for dealing with the world. He'd sit on my head.

And it didn't take hardly anything for Tyrone to figure I was doing him wrong. Like when he was about six ever' time it rained we'd go over and play house with Johnny Frances Woodham. And Johnny Frances always insisted that Tyrone be the baby 'cause she said he was so cute. So, we'd put Tyrone to bed in this big old crib they had and me and Johnny Frances would get in the big bed to play mama and daddy.

Pretty soon, Tyrone would poke his head up out of that crib and he'd say, "Harol', I'm gonna git you!" And sure enough, on the way home he'd throw me down in the rain and the mud and sit on my head. (*The general lights begin to soften leaving Hal in a spot that will dim under the following scene.*) Rainy days. Remember the sound of rain on a tin roof? (*We hear the first spatters of rain on metal.*) It would start off slow and then swell up till it was like a little engine. (*The sounds swell into a soft murmur.*) I suppose sometimes it would get really loud but I don't remember that.

PAPA

(*offstage*) Keep your voice down! No use in waking up your ma!

HAL

I used to wake up early in the morning and listen to the rain and see the grown-ups moving around in the gray light like bears coming out of their holes. (*Hal's light is very soft. He turns toward the kitchen as a sharp crack of thunder and a flash of light illuminate it for a moment. The lights come up over the kitchen area with the iron gray light of dawn. The sound of the rain is almost deafening for a moment and then fades under. Water begins to drip into a pan on the table. Kate enters the kitchen wearing her slip and rubbing sleep from her eyes. She looks out the screen door for a moment, shivers slightly although it is not cold, and moves to the stove. She opens the fire door, adds two sticks of firewood and a handful of kindling from the woodbox, and blows on the ashes. Satisfied the fire has started, she adjusts the damper and fills the coffee-pot with water from the pan on the table. Through all of this we are aware of her deep concern with the weather outside. Shivering again she strikes a match and "lights" the lamp. The stagelights brighten but the room is still filled with deep shadows. Taking an old suitcoat from a nail she puts it on, rubs more sleep from her eyes, and stoops to look into the skirted cupboard. There is the sound of feet scraping outside.*)

PAPA

(*offstage*) Git away, dammit! Git away! (*There is a cat squall followed by a loud thump. Kate rises and goes to the door.*)

KATE

You all right?

PAPA

(*offstage*) Yeah. (*Kate steps aside as Papa enters carrying a bucket and limping. He is a little more ragged than before and soaking wet.*) Ever' cat in the county's in that barn. Mind me to shoot a few of 'em 'fore night.

KATE

They're just hungry.

PAPA

Well, they scratch that cow's tits and there won't be no milk a-tall. Damn little now. (*He hands the bucket to Kate and she takes it to the cupboard. During the following she strains the milk through a cloth into a pitcher.*)

KATE

Why, Papa, there ain't more'n two quarts here.

PAPA

I know it. Like to not-a-had that. Four or five of them cats followed me right through the rain up to the house. Climbing right up my britches leg.

KATE

I heard one of them holler.

PAPA

I kicked the devil outten him!

KATE

What was that other racket I heard?

PAPA

I fell down. I come that close to spilling the milk! Mind me to go out yonder with the shotgun, hear?

KATE

You got any shells?

PAPA

(*remembering*) Oh. (*He pulls up a chair and sits at the table.*) Any coffee?

KATE

In a minute.

PAPA

Boy's up?

KATE

No, not yet.

PAPA

Might's well let 'im sleep. There ain't a stalk of cotton left standing on the place. This rain shore caught us just right. Another week or two and we'd-a made us a good crop. I ain't never seen cotton bearing any better. You got anything to eat in the stove?

KATE

No.

PAPA

A cold biscuit and a little grease will be all right. (*Kate doesn't answer.*)
I reckon that little Jersey's gonna go dry on us. Hurry up with that coffee, Kate. (*She finishes rinsing out the strainer cloth and hangs it on the
nail. She gets a cup and saucer from the cupboard, fills the cup, and puts
it before Papa.*) That looks mighty light. Hadn't you oughta run it
through again?

KATE

I don't think it'll help. It's the third day on them grounds. (*He shakes
some salt into the cup, stirs and saucers the coffee. He sips the coffee
with considerable noise. Kate pulls up a chair opposite Papa, sits and
watches him for a moment.*)

PAPA

What you staring at?

KATE

You want to know what they is in the house to eat?

PAPA

Kate, don't start in . .

KATE

They's two quarts of milk! (*Papa looks up expecting her to go on.*)
That's it!

PAPA

Now, don't get upsot. You always look at the short end of things. We'll
get something in here before dark. If nothing else I'll get us a mess of
squirrels.

KATE

You can't hunt squirrels in the rain without no shells.

PAPA

One of the boys can go down to the store . .

KATE

We ain't got no more credit!

PAPA

Keep your voice down! No use in waking up your ma!

KATE

We run outta credit in April. This is September! Tell me what you gonna
do! (*Papa rises, takes something from a shelf, takes out his pocketknife,*

sits down, and whittles.) Well?

PAPA

Hand me that matchstick, Kate. (*Kate shoves the matchstick across the table. Papa whittles on it and fastens it into the thing in his hands.*)

KATE

Mama's sick, Anna's done run off, you can't keep the boys here much longer; what you gonna do?

PAPA

I'm gonna tie a flatiron to your tongue and let you beat your brains out! Hush up and go on about your business.

KATE

I ain't thinking about me. I'm worried about Harol' and I'm worried about Mama. Mr. Paulk'll throw us outta here if you ain't made no crop and you know it! Now you can just sit right here whittling till doomsday but my mama's sick and that youngun's got to eat!

PAPA

You ain't got no call to set here and talk down to me like this. Ain't I always provided? When we had our own place didn't you have everything you wanted? Things are a little hard now but they'll pick up. Just hold your 'tater.

KATE

You lost that place in '22. You gotta forget about that and figure on to-day. How're things gonna pick up? Tell me how!

PAPA

You gonna "how" me right in the grave, ain't you? One of these days I'm gonna haul off and split your head. I wish you was one of the boys! I'd whip you good!

KATE

Just tell me how and I'll hush up.

PAPA

They's other places, Kate. All we gotta do is get through this coming winter. I was over at old man Stanley's 'tother day. He's got a nice section down by the river. Bottom land all the way.

KATE

Why that whole bank floods might nigh ever' year. You worse off there than you are here.

PAPA

There you go! It don't flood ever' year and the years it don't you can

153

make the best crop you ever seen down there. I talked to him and I think he'll let me have it.

KATE

What kinda terms?

PAPA

Same as this'n, a-course.

KATE

How's that? Eighteen dollars' credit and halves?

PAPA

Good as you can get. (*Kate shakes her head in frustration and disbelief, rises, and goes to the stove.*)

KATE

I don't mean to be mean to you. I reckon I oughta boil a little of this milk for Mama. (*She moves about putting milk into a pan and putting it on the stove. She hesitates before saying anything else.*) I know this is gonna make you mad but I gotta say it. You . . you oughta leave Mama alone. (*Papa's head snaps up and he stops whittling.*) She's sick, Papa. I heard you last night again. She's gotta have rest and something to eat! You can't . . do that! You gonna kill her! (*Papa stands and for a moment it looks as though he is going to hit her. Finally . .*)

PAPA

You got your nose into ever'thing, ain't you? (*He puts the knife in his pocket and holds out his hand.*) Give me the coat. (*She gives him the coat and he puts it on.*)

KATE

What you gonna do?

PAPA

First thing I'm gonna do is not pay you no mind. (*She turns back to the stove.*) You reckon that's right about the boys leaving?

KATE

You know Edlo wants to get married and Hub already spends all his time up at Troy now. I 'speck the others will be right behind. Why?

PAPA

Looks like me and Harol'll be the only roosters left in the hen house, don't it? I swear I'm glad they ain't all like you. (*He settles his hat on his head and moves toward the door.*)

KATE

What you gonna do?

PAPA

I'm going in to town. Might be some hauling or something somebody wants done. (*He starts out the door. Kate picks up the object he was whittling on. It is a little paddle wheel.*)

KATE

You want me to put this up?

PAPA

Naw, I'm through with it. Tell Harol' I made him a flutter mill. That gully down by the barn is just right for a flutter mill today. (*He pulls down his hat and hunkers into his coat and exits through the screen door. Offstage*) Git outta here, you damn cats! (*There is a cat squall followed by a loud thump. Kate goes to the door and looks out.*)

KATE

You all right?

PAPA

(*offstage*) Yeah. (*She comes back to the table and idly spins the toy in her hands. She looks at the lamp as it sputters and dies. She sighs, moves the pan of milk from the stove, and exits into the wings calling softly.*)

KATE

Harol'? Harol'! Wake up, shug. Look what Papa made you. (*The lights on the kitchen fade out as Hal's spot brightens followed by the general lights.*)

HAL

Talking about rain, my granddaddy used to make the best flutter mills. After a rain I'd have a flutter mill in ever' gully on the place. Then old Tyrone Price would come over and sit on 'em.

So, that's the way I growed up. Trying not to be best friends with Tyrone Price. I kept trying to avoid him but it was hard. He kept growing like a big watermelon. You couldn't look down the road without seeing him . .

PAPA

(*offstage*) This big old bear was after me . . (*Hal reacts with slight surprise to the voice, then smiling, he continues.*)

HAL

Oh. Well, that's what Tyrone Price was like; a big old bear.

PAPA

(*offstage*) That old bear scared off the dogs . .

HAL

Papa, could you wait a minute? I'm talking about Tyrone Price.

PAPA

(*offstage*) I couldn't even climb a tree. He was right behind me . .

HAL

(*ruefully*) I guess you'll have to wait to hear any more about Tyrone Price. (*The lights are changing, coming up on the porch area. It is day-time. Papa comes around the house talking as though Hal is walking at his side. He is dressed much the same as before but there should be some change to indicate the passage of time. Papa moves to the edge of the porch and Hal joins him and sits on the steps where he will remain throughout the scene. In the scene Papa never loses his bravado and his humor. It is not that he is unfeeling but life must be met on terms that allow life to continue.*)

PAPA

Well, sir, this old bear chased me about four mile and then he cornered me. (*He pauses for effect.*) Then the old bear come right up to me and he opened his mouth about this wide. (*Papa gestures a mouth that is enormous. Again he pauses. Hal is mesmerized.*) So I seen my chance and I caught that old bear by the nose and I stuck my shotgun down his throat and I shot him!

HAL

Did you kill him?

PAPA

Not right off, but I filled him so full of holes that he just stood there awhile and drained hisself to death!

HAL

He did?

PAPA

Yeah. I been using his hide ever since to keep my money in.

HAL

Papa, can I have a penny?

PAPA

Papa ain't got no penny, shug.

HAL

You said you kept your money in a bearskin.

PAPA

That's right, hon. But you remember all them holes? Papa had a penny but it fell outten a hole and I lost it.

HAL

Oh. Papa, was it a boy bear or a girl bear?

PAPA

I don't know, why?

HAL

I don't know how to tell boy bears from girl bears.

PAPA

You don't? Same as you tell for ever'body else.

HAL

Mama wears a dress . .

PAPA

That ain't how. Didn't I ever tell you the difference? (*Hal shakes his head.*) Well, you listen. Don't you ever forget this and you'll know. When God made a man he left a string hanging out. (*Very unsuggestively Papa pantomimes a penislike string with his finger.*) When God made a woman his string ran out. (*With his fingers he pantomimes a circle.*) You see?

HAL

Nossir.

PAPA

Well, you see, a little boy . . (*Kate has appeared at the screen door and has heard this last. She is dressed in a very faded, worn version of the first dress she wore.*)

KATE

I didn't know you'all was back.

HAL

Mama, Papa told me how to tell a boy bear from a girl bear.

PAPA

Hush, shug.

KATE

What you telling him now?

PAPA

Nothing, Kate. Go on about your business.

KATE

You sell them watermelons?

PAPA

Naw.

KATE

You didn't? You took that whole wagon load over there.

157

PAPA

Yeah, well, they didn't want no watermelons.

KATE

Papa, we need that money.

PAPA

Dammit! I told you they didn't want no watermelons!

HAL

Mama, we throwed them all to the hogs.

PAPA

Hush.

KATE

You feed all them watermelons to the hogs?

PAPA

Hush, Harol'. Kate, I told you to go on about your business.

KATE

Mama's lying in there waiting for you! You said you was going to sell them watermelons and go by Dr. Waters's and . .

PAPA

Dammit, I don't want to hear about it! (*There is a long pause while Kate assesses the situation. She has moved out on the porch and now she sits in the chair.*)

KATE

Why didn't they want no watermelons? (*Papa doesn't answer.*) You'd think anybody would want them watermelons. I don't remember you ever having a better year for 'em. Wasn't like last year when we got rained out. Best year I ever seen for melons. (*Kate's more moderate attitude begins to draw Papa out.*)

PAPA

Yeah, they wanted them, but . .

KATE

(*gently*) What happened?

PAPA

Sister, them are stubborn men. I figured to get ten cents apiece on them melons. You know there wasn't a one of 'em under fifty pound. I figured with that whole wagonload I'd get two — three dollars. It's hot down in that cut where they're building that trustle. Damn near busted the wagon getting down there.

HAL

Papa had to pry us outten a hole . .

KATE

Hush, Harol'.

PAPA

They offered me twenty-five cents for the whole load.

KATE

All them melons?

PAPA

That what they said. They said twenty-five cents or nothing. And they was betting among theyselves that I couldn't even get the wagon outta there loaded down like it was. I told them I'd feed them watermelons to the hogs first.

HAL

Papa let me help.

KATE

So you come back here and throwed 'em to the hogs. You could've took 'em to town. You might'uv sold some.

PAPA

I said I'd throw 'em to the hogs. (*Kate doesn't approve what Papa has done but she understands why he did it.*)

KATE

Mama's just lying there looking like she's gonna bust. Maybe if I went to the drugstore and talked to Mr. Dean . .

PAPA

It'll be like them watermelons, Kate.

KATE

I know.

HAL

Mama, Papa's got a whole bearskin full of money.

KATE

He has? Papa, you oughten to tell Harol' about bears. You got him scared to death.

PAPA

Don't be scared of no bears, shug.

HAL

I heard a bear last night.

KATE

I told you, that was Papa snoring. (*Kate has been making a decision. She rises and speaks directly to Papa.*) I'm gonna get a job. In town. I could

159

work at the café. (*This is obviously an argument of long standing. Papa looks at her evenly.*)

PAPA

I told you I don't want none of my younguns working in town. (*Kate just looks at him and turns to go inside. We hear the long mournful whistle of the cotton mill. Kate pauses as she hears it, then speaks to no one in particular.*)

KATE

I'd sure hate to work in that cotton mill. (*Kate moves on into the house.*)

PAPA

Did you think Papa's snoring was a bear? Papa snores to keep them bears away. (*Papa stands, looks at the weather, then turns to go inside.*) You play quiet now. Your granny's sick. (*He pauses for a moment with the door open and laughs.*) Well, we won't have to feed them hogs tonight! (*Papa goes inside and gently closes the screen door.*) (*The lights have begun to change back to the way they were before the scene. Hal becomes aware of the audience.*)

HAL

Where was I? Bears . . hogs . . oh, yes. Tyrone Price. Always sitting on my head. The only defense I had against old Tyrone was to let him listen to our radio. (*Hal moves over to the radio on the cupboard and turns it on.*)

KATE

(*offstage*) Why was you crying today?

HAL

The scariest part was waiting for it to warm up. I didn't know if Tyrone was gonna sit on me or the floor.

KATE

(*offstage*) I musta heard you crying thirty times today. (*Hal picks up the radio and moves back toward the porch as though to get away from the voices.*)

HAL

(*ruefully*) Give a memory an inch and it'll take a mile. I never knew why but my mama bought us a radio when we didn't have too much else. And we had the only radio around. I remember Papa had to string an aerial clean across the sass-garden. (*He puts the radio on the porch.*) We didn't even have electricity back then and Papa did the strangest thing. The power line between Opp and Florala ran right near our house so Papa hung a old bedspring to the nearest power pole and run a wire from the bedspring to the radio and it worked just dandy. The oddest thing happened about that radio. The country people for miles around would come over to our yard ever' evening and stand in groups near the window where the radio was. All I can remember is the silent men in their overalls and hats, not smiling, not frowning; just standing there listening to something they had never heard and probably couldn't imagine. (*Static is heard.*) Uh-oh. Here it comes. (*Hal tunes the dial back and forth.*)

KATE

(*offstage*) I'm gonna make you a promise. A real promise!

HAL

Not now! (*Hal tunes a moment more and the static fades into the radio program — see the Supplementary Material at the end of the play. Hal grins at the audience, picks up his guitar and tries to play along.*)

KATE

(*offstage*) Harol'! (*The general lighting is fading to darkness while the kitchen lights come up with the soft light of a summer's late afternoon. Kate walks into the scene pulling a simple ragged housedress over a tattered slip. About a year and a half has passed since we last saw her. All the brightness is gone. She looks tired and swollen as though she just waked from unsatisfactory sleep. Her feet and legs hurt her so that she has a slight limp. Hal ignores all this and tries to keep the audience's attention.*)

HAL

I used to think ever'body learned to play the guitar by playing along with the radio. The big problem was being in tune. I was afraid to retune too much; you broke a string you had to send clean to Montgomery for a new one.

KATE

Harol'!

HAL

I guess just about my favorite program was "Little Jimmy and His Dad."

KATE

Harol'!

HAL

Ever'body loved Little Jimmy.

KATE

Harol'!

HAL

If I could-a been anybody I wanted to, I'd-a been Little Jimmy.

KATE

Harol', you answer me! Harol', you better answer me! Now you come away from that radio and put down that ukulele! Harol'! Do you hear me?

HAL

(*reluctantly*) Yes, Mama.

KATE

Harol', you turn that radio off and come in here!

HAL

Yes'm. (*The radio sound stops abruptly and putting the guitar down, Hal walks directly into the scene and sits at the table. During the course of the following scene Kate puts on anklets and rolls them down to her anklebone, puts on her heavy work shoes, pins her hair into a bun, makes a lunch of a couple of biscuits, and prepares to leave for work at the cotton mill. Interspersed with this she makes a small effort to clean up the table and sweep a few crumbs away.*)

KATE

I can't find my snuffbox. You been playing with my snuffbox again?

HAL

No'm.

KATE

Lord-a-mercy! What am I gonna do with you? All day long when I'm trying to sleep you're taking ever'thing out in the yard to play with it. Now, where is my snuff?

HAL

I didn't mess with your snuffbox, Mama. All I played with today was the strainer.

KATE

My strainer? (*She rises and looks quickly into the cupboard.*) What was you doing with my strainer?

HAL

Me and Bonnie Faye was just sifting some sand. (*Kate can't find her strainer anywhere in the kitchen.*)

KATE

Well, where is my strainer? Now I can't find that. Harol', do you hear me? Where is my strainer?

HAL

It fell in the privy, Mama. We didn't mean for it to fall in. Bonnie Faye said she'd give us her mama's strainer.

KATE

I declare, I don't know what I'm gonna do with you.

HAL

I'm sorry, Mama.

KATE

You've lost my snuff, my strainer, and I'm afraid to find out what else. I don't know why I even try to sleep. What was you crying about? I musta heard you crying thirty times today. I told Mr. Lee at the school you wasn't no crybaby and that's why he's gonna let you start to school a year early. But if you're gonna be a crybaby . .

HAL

I don't want to start to school, Mama. I rather . .

KATE

Now, you hush! There's no reason why you can't start to school. Rose has already taught you your pluses and your take-a-ways and you can walk to school with Tyrone Price and . .

HAL

Mama, Tyrone sits on me!

KATE

Now, you hush, you hear? You being a crybaby again. Tyrone Price is a nice boy. He may be a little rough but you have to learn to stand up to him. You don't want to be a scardey-cat.

HAL

Aw, Mama, Tyrone is so big. (*Kate has been moving slowly about the kitchen and now picks up a soiled canvas apron with large pockets. Her hand strikes something in the pocket.*)

KATE

Oh, here's my snuff. It was in my work apron. (*During the following she opens the small snuff can, shakes a small amount of snuff into the lid, and carefully places the snuff inside her lower lip.*) Praise the Lord for snuff! I declare, I don't know how I'd do it without my snuff. (*She looks about under the table.*) Now, where's my spit can? You and Bonnie Faye probably dropped that in the privy, too. (*She finds her spit can, a soup can or something similar, spits into it, and places it conveniently near by.*) Well, you got to go to school. You want to be like me? Working twelve hours a night in that cotton mill and trying to sleep in the day-time? And ever'time you get something nice your youngun drops it in the privy?

KATE

HAL

No, Mama, but you ain't supposed to start to school till you're six.

KATE

Why, Harol', you can already read as good as anybody. Is that what you want to be? A rent farmer just like the rest of this family? A rent farmer? Never have nothing, never know nothing? Look how messy they are. (*She indicates the cluttered table which she has unsuccessfully tidied up.*) They don't even clean up after theyselves. Why do you think I bought that radio? So you could learn to play the ukulele? No. I want you to know more'n us. Now, you listen. I'm gonna make you a promise. A *real* promise. (*Hal's interest has lagged and he is now involved in a crack in the oilcloth.*) Are you listening?

HAL

Yes'm.

KATE

Ever' year you pass I'm gonna put a dollar away for you. Then when you finish school you'll have twelve dollars and you can buy yourself a nice suit. And you know what I want you to do? I'm gonna talk to Mr. Dean about it. You could work at the drugstore in Opp. Just like Blan Stanley. Wouldn't that be nice? (*Hal nods.*) And you could wear your suit and sell co-colers (*Coca-Colas*) and maybe even mix medicines. You know I won't be able to work at that cotton mill forever. My legs are bothering me already. And when I'm old, why you could look after me. (*Hal's interest has lagged again.*) Now you promise me you'll be Mama's little man. I gotta go to work now but I want you to promise me you'll eat your supper and you'll go to bed and not make any trouble for your granny. And you'll leave that radio alone!

HAL

Yes'm.

KATE

Just think. You'd work at the drugstore and maybe people would call you "Mr. Ryan." You know, ever'body always called your daddy "Mr. Ryan." (*In the distance the cotton mill whistle is heard; two long, low blasts. Kate rises with a sigh and completes her preparations. With her lunch, her apron, and her sweater she moves toward the door.*) I'm sorry about the snuffbox, honey, but I don't know what I'll do about the strainer. I wouldn't want to use it now anyway . . (*Kate exits through the screen door. Hal looks after her for a moment and the radio sound fades up. Hal smiles at the audience, stands, goes over to the cupboard and rummages about. He finds a pitcher of buttermilk and a clean glass. He smells the buttermilk and goes back to his seat at the table.*)

HAL

Ever' mother in the south loved Little Jimmy. Ever' one except mine. Mama always wanted us to listen to what she called "classical music" from the Mobile station. Songs like "Pennies from Heaven" and "Love Letters in the Sand." But as soon as she'd leave for work, we'd turn on Little Jimmy.

One night though, we was all sitting around listening to Mama's "good music" and lightning struck the aerial and that little old radio just exploded. Papa was yawning at the time and one of the knobs hit him right in the mouth. After ever'thing settled down and we got the fire out in the radio and the knob outten Papa's throat, Papa said, "I thought I might be wrong about Kate's music but now I know I'm right. Even God Almighty don't like it!" (*Hal chuckles and pours a glass of buttermilk from the pitcher.*) How long has it been since you had a glass of buttermilk? (*As he drinks, the stage fades to darkness. The radio continues to play as the houselights come up.*)

INTERMISSION

ACT TWO

The houselights dim to darkness but the intermission music continues, softening with the houselights until it is like a half-heard radio. The objects on stage are silhouetted. Hal walks through a screen door and moves to a table where there is an oil lamp. He adjusts the lamp and the stagelights come up as before. Again Hal's grin invites the audience to share in the theatrical deception. The stage is filled with sets depicting two different scenes. One is a porch, this time with a porch swing and an old straight chair. On the steps are a pocketknife, some pieces of wood, a hammer, and a half-completed wooden airplane made from a cedar cigar box. Shavings are scattered about the steps. The screen door and the steps are in different places from the porch in the first act. A scraggly geranium struggles for life in a clay pot. The other set is a small kitchen. There is a window with a broken shutter but no glass and the inevitable screen door. There is a new coal-oil stove, a pine table with two chairs, a small cupboard with a faded skirt. On the cupboard is a bucket and a porcelain pan. A small mirror hangs from a string. Against one wall sits a cheap metal trunk that is used for a chair, table, or whatever. On the pine table is the radio we saw earlier and this is where the music is coming from. The lamp is also on the table and the guitar leans against the table's side. Both these sets should indicate different houses as in the first act. Many of the same set pieces can be used with different accessories, etc. When the lights come up we see that Hal is carrying his half-finished glass of buttermilk.

HAL

Did you go out and get some buttermilk? (*He drains his glass, puts it on the table, and looks about.*) Look what we done while you were out. (*He moves over to the porch and again places a roof support into place, looking up as though seeing a porch roof, reminiscent of the first act. One last look about and he is ready to begin. The music swells up momentarily and Hal acknowledges it with a look and then sits in the swing.*) Well, the radio wasn't the only modern convenience that come to Opp. When I was about nine or ten we begun to get airplanes. 'Course we didn't have a airport or anything like that but we did have an awful lot of pasture. And ever' now and then some barnstormer would land his plane and try to sell rides. First two or three times people just stood around and throwed clods of dirt at them. Later on we'd go right up to the fence.

PAPA

(*offstage*) He had his hairlip hooked over her carbuncle . .

HAL

(*annoyed*) Oh. Yes.

PAPA

(*offstage*) He had his hairlip hooked over her carbuncle . .

HAL

I guess good taste ain't absolutely essential to a memory, is it?

PAPA

(*offstage*) He had his hairlip . .

HAL

Fine! Let me tell it my way, okay? (*Hal moves over to the steps and begins hammering on the airplane during the following speech. He will remain here during the scene. The stagelights isolate the porch in fading light. The radio fades out and we hear the sounds of crickets.*) But I loved them airplanes right from the start. Rickety old things. The aviators all wore them funny leather caps with the goggles. You could buy little cheap ones in town made out of oilcloth with celluloid goggles. Ever' kid in Opp had one and we went ever'where with our goggles *down.* (*Hal turns his full attention to the airplane.*)

KATE

(*offstage*) Harol'! (*Hal doesn't respond.*) Harol'! (*no response*) Harol', you outside?

HAL

(*still working*) Yes'm! (*Kate is seen behind the screen door.*)

KATE

(*offstage*) Oh, there you are. (*no response*) What you doing?

HAL

Making something.

KATE

(*offstage*) Don't you want to listen to the radio?

HAL

No'm, it ain't working.

KATE

(*offstage*) It ain't? How come?

HAL

The aerial broke.

KATE

(*offstage*) Oh. (*There is a pause.*) What you making?

HAL

Airplane.

KATE

(*offstage*) Oh. (*Kate pauses again.*) You gonna hurt your eyes. (*The screen door opens and Kate steps out onto the porch. She is a little tired looking but very pulled together. Her hair is cut in a bob and curled. She is wearing lipstick, rouge, and earrings. There is even lipstick on the ball of her little finger where she has smoothed it on her lips. She has on fingernail polish but her nails are very short. Her dress is cheap but "dressy" and she wears stockings with seams. Her stockings are held up by elastic garters rolled just above her knee. Frequently during the scene*

167

she will pull the stockings taut by pulling at the garters through the dress. Her dress hem is considerably below her knees. As she comes to the edge of the porch she looks off as though expecting someone to come up the road.) Time to start cleaning up your mess, honey.

HAL

In a minute.

KATE

Don't leave none of them little nails on the steps. (*Something in the sound of her voice makes Hal look up and he sees her for the first time. He laughs.*)

HAL

You look funny. (*Kate nervously covers her mouth with her hand for a moment.*)

KATE

Now you hush! You know what lipstick is. (*She moves into the yard still watching the road with expectancy.*) It's nice to get dressed up a little on Saturday night. I wish I could get you to do it. (*Hal ignores this and picks up a piece of wood. During the rest of the scene he will carve a propeller for the plane.*) Why don't you go 'round back and pick some hollyhocks for Sunday school tomorrow? I bet Mrs. Scofield would like a big bunch of hollyhocks. (*no response*) Harol'!

HAL

Yes'm, in a minute. (*Kate moves back on the porch and dusts the swing seat.*)

KATE

Why don't you do it now?

HAL

Mama, can I go to the picture show next Saturday?

KATE

I don't know. What's playing? (*She sits on the swing and carefully arranges her skirt.*)

HAL

Bob Steele.

KATE

(*absently*) Hm-m-m.

HAL

It's supposed to be a good one.

KATE

If I say you can go will you clean up that mess and go cut them flowers and get ready for bed? It's almost dark.

HAL

You mean I can go?

KATE

I didn't say that. We'll see. Come on now! I'm tired of asking you. Pick it all up . . (*Kate is interrupted by the loud laughter of men inside the house. One voice we recognize as Papa's; the other is a big slow, "Haw! Haw! Haw!" She looks nervously from the screen door to the road.*)

PAPA

(*offstage*) So he said, "Throw a bucket of water on 'em. He's got his hair-lip hooked over her carbuncle!" (*This is followed by an explosion of laughter.*)

MAN

(*offstage trying to catch his breath*) That's a good'un, Mr. Bird! It shore is! I better remember that 'un for paw! Yessir!

KATE

(*apprehensively*) Harol', go see who that is.

HAL

Yes'm. (*He starts to get up but stops when he hears . .*)

MAN

(*offstage*) 'Scuse me, Mr. Bird. I come over to set with Kate. Is she home?

PAPA

(*offstage*) Yeah. She's probably on the piazer. I think she's expecting you.

HAL

(*overlapping*) I know who that is.

MAN

(*offstage*) Haw! Haw! Haw! Much obliged. I'll tell paw you was asking about him.

KATE

(*a little angry*) Never mind, so do I. (*A man is seen at the screen door.*)

MAN

(*offstage*) Throw a bucket of water on 'em. His hairlip is hooked over her carbuncle! Haw! Haw! Haw! (*The door opens and Hobe — rhymes with Toby — a large, slouchy man comes onto the porch. His overalls are new and sharply creased where they were folded. He has on a clean striped*

*shirt and a suit vest. His hat is a brown hunter's cap with earflaps, very
much the worse for wear. His shoes and half his pant leg are covered with
a red sticky clay. If the actor can manage it he should be chewing tobacco or dipping snuff. Spitting is a problem onstage but the potted plant
would make an excellent cuspidor. If he is using tobacco, juice will be
running down both sides of his mouth to his chin. Hobe is not offensive,
just comically undesirable.)* Hi-di, Kate. Good evening to you.

KATE

(a little tight) Hey, Hobe. I didn't know you was here. You must have
pulled in the back 'fore I come out.

HOBE

Well, I — Haw! Haw! Haw! — I come in the back door, all right.

KATE

My goodness, I must be losing my hearing. I didn't even hear the car.

HOBE

The car? Aw, naw, I walked over. Through the pasture. We been losing
so many guinea hens I thought I might find some nests.

KATE

Walked over?

HOBE

Yeah, looking for nests.

KATE

(looking at his shoes) Did you find any?

HOBE

Naw! Haw! Haw! I reckon they're too smart for me. Haw! Haw! Haw!
*(Hobe finally becomes aware that Kate is looking at his feet. He looks
down and sees the mud.)* Well, look at my shoes. I reckon I tracked that
right through the house. Haw! Haw! Haw! *(Kate clenches her teeth.)*

KATE

That's all right, Hobe. It sweeps up pretty good. *(under her breath)*
When it's dry. *(There is a pause as Hobe attempts to scrape a little of the
mud from his shoes on the edge of the porch. Mud on shoes or floors is
not one of the important things to Hobe. Trying to rescue the moment,
Kate makes room for Hobe on the swing.)* Sit down, Hobe. *(Hobe giggles
and guffaws embarrassedly.)*

HOBE

Why, much obliged, don't mind if I do! *(He clumps over the rocker and*

drags it to the swing. Overcome at the sight of Kate he turns to Hal.)
Hey!

HAL

Hey, Hobe.

KATE

Why, Harol', stand up when you say "hey." (*Hal rises to his knees and puts out his hand.*)

HAL

Hey, Hobe. (*Hal catches Kate's eye.*) Uh . . Mr. Gilchrest. (*They shake hands solemnly.*)

HOBE

Hey, Harol'. What you making?

HAL

Airplane.

HOBE

(*excitedly*) Yeah?

KATE

Yes, he's got the cowboy and airplane fever. (*directly at Hal*) He was just about to go cut some flowers for Sunday school. (*sweetly*) Hobe, I I thought you was driving over. (*Hobe fascinated by the toy airplane.*)

HOBE

Airplane? You see that airplane that landed in old man Spurlin's pasture?

HAL

When?

KATE

Hobe, didn't you say you was bringing your car?

HAL

When was it, Hobe?

HOBE

I think it was a week ago Tuesday. Feller was selling rides.

KATE

(*loudly*) Hobe?

HAL

He was?

HOBE

(*the big joke payoff*) Yeah. He didn't say where they was riding to! Haw! Haw! Haw! (*more seriously*) It shore was a big thing. Had a motor on it.

171

KATE

(*yelling*) Hobe!

HOBE

Yeah?

HAL

Boy, howdy! Mama, can I . .

KATE

Harol', hush! Hobe, didn't you say you was bringing your car?

HOBE

I did?

KATE

You said we was going for a ride this evening.

HAL

Mama, can I . . (*Hobe moves back onto the porch.*)

HOBE

I reckon I forgot. Where was we a-going to?

KATE

It don't matter where we was going to . .

HAL

Mama . . (*Hobe sits heavily in the chair.*)

HOBE

Well, I just as soon sit here . .

KATE

You can go back and get the car, Hobe.

HAL

Mama, can I . .

KATE

(*trying to remain calm*) Hush, Harol', and go inside.

HOBE

You mean walk all the way back to the house?

KATE

It won't take but a minute. I'd give a pretty to get out of the house for a while. We might even have a little fun. (*Hobe suddenly remembers and is relieved.*)

HOBE

Wouldn't do no good to walk back to the house. Paw took the front wheels off the car and put them on the wagon.

HAL

Mama, can I go over to old man . .

KATE

(*exploding*) I told you to hush and get inside!

HOBE

Now, don't be upsot, Kate. I figured we'd have a good time right here. (*He stands and speaks confidentially.*) I brought something to perk us up. Haw! Haw! Haw! (*He pats his overall pocket confidently. Then, in surprise, he checks all his pockets.*)

KATE

(*nervously*) Hobe!

HOBE

Damn! I had it!

KATE

Not now, Hobe! (*She calls loudly.*) Papa! Papa! Would you make Harol' come in!

HAL

What kind was it, Hobe?

HOBE

(*still searching*) Store bought! I gave two dollars for that!

HAL

I mean the airplane, Hobe. (*Hobe is still half standing searching his pockets.*)

HOBE

I don't know, Harol', but it had a motor on it. (*to Kate*) Kate, I swear I had it.

KATE

(*very firm*) Harol', clean up them steps and go cut them hollyhocks! (*She calls loudly.*) Papa!

HAL

Yes'm. (*The screen door opens and Papa steps out. He is dressed only in summer BVD's and a straw hat.*)

PAPA

Hey, Hobe. What you squalling about, Kate?

KATE

Papa, I just want Harol' . .

HOBE

Mr. Bird, did you see my bottle? (*Papa hands Hobe an empty half-pint whiskey bottle.*)

PAPA

Oh, yeah, Hobe. Much obliged. I finished that off. Just did. Thank you.

HAL

Papa, Hobe seen a real airplane!

PAPA

He did? When did he?

KATE

Harol' get in the house! (*We now notice that Papa is holding his finger.*)

PAPA

Kate, where is the Mercurochrome? I cut my finger on that bottle!

KATE

On the mantel! And take this youngun with you!

PAPA

Harol', come inside!

HAL

Yessir. (*Hal slowly begins to clean up the mess as Papa goes back inside. After a moment Hal sees that he has been forgotten so he resumes his whittling.*)

HOBE

I'm sorry about the bottle, Kate.

KATE

That's all right, Hobe. Just sit down. I can always fix some coffee.

HOBE

I guess I left it there in the house when I was a-talking to your paw. Thought he might like a little drink on my way through. (*Kate is very anxious to change the conversation.*)

KATE

How's your mama, Hobe? I don't never see her in town no more.

HOBE

Maw? She's all right, thank you. Did your paw drink that whole bottle? (*He squints at the bottle hoping to see one drop.*)

KATE

Tell her I'll be pleased to walk to town with her next Saturday if she's going in.

HOBE

Aw, she won't be going. She purely hates Opp. Says she ain't gonna set foot in it. Haw! Haw! Says she wants to be buried in the backyard. Says it's too crowded in Opp. Says all's they wants is her money.

KATE

(*still trying*) Well, I can't argue that. (*Kate tries to make a little joke.*)

174

'Bout the best thing about Opp is it's just three miles to Poley. (*She laughs, trying to get Hobe to join in.*)

HOBE

Poley? There ain't nothing in Poley 'cepting that old sawmill.

KATE

Oh, I know that, Hobe. It was just a little joke.

HOBE

Sawmill don't even work no more. Last time I was to Poley there was pine trees growing in the middle of the road.

KATE

It was just a joke, Hobe!

HOBE

Oh! Haw! Haw! A joke! Your paw just told me a funny one! Haw! Haw! It's about this old woman who had a carbuncle and this old man who had a hairlip . .

KATE

(*desperately*) Harol', go ask your granny to heat up the coffee, shug . . (*The screen door bangs open. Papa is standing there, waving his finger and blowing on it.*)

PAPA

Kate, what in the hell kind of Mercurochrome is this?

KATE

I reckon it's the same old kind . .

PAPA

Well, it ain't! I think I'm pizzened!

KATE

Let me see the bottle. (*Papa hands the small bottle to Kate and she squints at it.*) This is fingernail polish! You got the wrong bottle!

PAPA

Well, it looked like Mercurochrome to me. Damn! It burns!

KATE

Good!

PAPA

Say what?

KATE

Go ask Rossy to put some remover on it. Hurry, before it dries!

PAPA

What is the fingernail polish doing on the mantel? What if I'd took a swallow of that?

175

KATE

It probably wouldn't hurt you. Rossy can get it off! (*Papa bangs off yelling at the top of his voice.*)

PAPA

Rossy! Rossy May! Come here! (*Hobe has been oblivious to all that has been going on.*)

HOBE

I hope you ain't upsot about that bottle, Kate. We can still have a pretty good time if you want to. (*Hobe leans over and gives Kate a big wink culminated by a spit into the geranium.*)

KATE

I don't care about your bottle or his finger or anything. I just wanted to go for a ride! (*Her eye catches Hal busily whittling.*) And you!

HOBE

Aw, let him set with us a minute, Kate. I never really got to know your boy. I see him going by the house, lickety-split to town, that cotton-top just a-flying. Where do you go ever' morning?

HAL

To school, Hobe.

HOBE

Oh, yeah. Haw! Haw! I forgot about that. (*Hobe takes a package of Camel cigarettes from his pocket.*)

HOBE

Want a ready roll?

HAL

(*looking at Kate*) Nossir.

KATE

Why, he's not old enough to smoke cigarettes.

HOBE

He ain't? (*to Hal*) How old are you?

HAL

Nine and a half.

HOBE

That's plenty old. Here, take one. (*Hal reaches eagerly.*)

KATE

Hobe! Harol'! (*The screen door bangs open once again and Papa appears. His finger is now wrapped in a rag and he has his overalls on.*)

PAPA

Hobe! Did you leave down that fence by the pasture?

HOBE

Damn! I might'uv. How come? (*Papa pushes Hobe's shoulder, Hobe rises obligingly, and Papa takes the seat.*)

PAPA

Old man Hardage's big Guernsey just come in the backyard. Must'uv et her way right through the corn!

HOBE

Damn, I'm sorry, Mr. Bird. Old man Hardage lets that cow roam all over. She's a good cow, too.

PAPA

I know it! Kate, how many times has she been over here?

KATE

Four or five times. Did you speak to Mr. Hardage?

PAPA

'Course I did! I told him he owed me fifty foot of fence and 'bout twenty bushels of corn!

HOBE

Haw! Haw! What'd he say to that?

PAPA

Told me to go to hell! That old fool! I oughta fix him good!

KATE

Now, Papa.

HOBE

Why don't you tie her up and milk her for a while. I hear she's a champeen milker.

PAPA

Naw. He'd have the law on me.

HOBE

Well, get the law on him!

PAPA

(*thinking*) Naw! . . Hobe, you ever spay a cow?

HOBE

Spay a cow? Haw! Haw! You can't spay a cow!

KATE

Papa, he'll shoot you!

PAPA

We was to spay her and keep her shut up in the barn a couple of days, he'd never know!

177

HOBE

We spay her she won't never give another drop of milk! Haw! Haw!

PAPA

Won't his face fall when she comes paddling home, dry as a board?

HOBE

Let's do 'er!

KATE

Papa! Hobe!

PAPA

It'll be just like spaying a big old hog! Come on, Hobe! While it's still light!

HOBE

I'm with you, Mr. Bird! Count me in! (*Papa and Hobe exit excitedly around the corner of the house.*)

PAPA

(*offstage*) Last time she'll eat my corn!

HOBE

(*offstage*) Won't his face drop? (*Hal grins and leans around the house to see into the backyard. After a moment he glances at Kate and then realizes how important this evening was to her. Finally . . *)

HAL

Mama, I know that joke Hobe was going to tell you. (*Kate stands and looks at Hal as though he is a stranger.*)

KATE

Good. (*She moves absently toward the door.*) I think I'll go in. Don't stay up too late. (*She walks vacantly through the door pulling the earrings into her hands. Hal sits for a moment looking after Kate.*)

PAPA

(*offstage*) Hold her, Hobe! Dammit, hold her!

HOBE

(*offstage*) I'm trying, Mr. Bird! Look out, she's getting away! (*Hal laughs, looks at the audience, and spins the propeller he has fastened to the toy. He rises and moves down to the audience.*)

HAL

Well, them aviators come and they went and nobody ever did take a ride. Finally, one of them musta really needed the money 'cause he cut his price to two dollars and fifty cents. That begun to sound pretty attractive so several of the businessmen chipped in and bought a ticket. For the mayor. Well, pore feller, he didn't want to go but he couldn't rightly back out. So he tied his hat on and climbed in. If you'd-a cut his throat he wouldn'a bled a drop. They took off and they was gone about fifteen minutes and then they come sailing back in. The mayor got out, shaking like a leaf. He had throwed up all over his seersucker suit. He hated to look like a sissy so he climbed up on a stump, looked out over the crowd, and said, "Friends, things are bad. We got a mighty sick-looking town!" (*The radio has crept back on. Hal takes note of it, turns it off, and moves it over to the porch.*)

You ever turn your radio on late at night and listen to the preachers? One faith healer I heard the other night kept saying, "Put one hand on the radio and the other hand up to God and promise you'll send me five dollars and you'll feel better, friends! And to really get well, send ten dollars! Do it now, friends, do it now!" I'll admit I felt a little silly standing there like that but I did feel better when I sent him his five dollars. I felt even better when he sent me a full-color, life-size photograph of Jesus that stands on its own feet. There's even a little place in the back to put Mercurochrome that drips out the front like blood. It's the best thing I got in my whole house. Ever'body wants to see it.

But the best faith healers I ever saw was the ones that used to come to Opp ever' year. They had the biggest tent! It filled that whole vacant lot between the post office and the municipal building. And it had lights all around the outside and benches inside and sawdust on the ground and a big open place in the back for the folks that was too sick to sit on the benches. And up front was a great big old purple velvet curtain with a picture of Jesus on it all worked out with sparkley stuff and old Jesus was just-a smiling down on ever'body.

And you know, sick folks would come from all over. It made it kinda like a holiday and we'd all stand on the street and watch the different families coming in. Some of the pore folks couldn't even get out of bed and they'd have to be toted along in their bedsteads. A particular nice quilt or a hand-crotcheted bedspread would always get a lot of "oh's" and "ah's" and maybe even some applause.

And of course, some of them would be on crutches or be pulled in coaster wagons. The best one I ever saw was a woman who stuffed her sick husband in a old oil drum and rolled him all the way from Fleeter, which was about eight mile.

Anyway, about dark, all them lights would go on outside and we'd start lining up to get in. There was a feller at the door selling fans and little

Bibles and medals and cotton candy and things like that and once you got past him you had to fight for a seat because the best place was right up front. That way you didn't miss a thing.

And then, just as ever'body was settling down, fanning and trying to get a little elbow room, the lights up over the stage would start blinking on and off. Then a whole bunch of colored lights would come on right over old Jesus' face and they spelled out, "ELSIE, JACK, AND JIM." While we was applauding the lights, "POP!" out they'd step from behind that curtain!

All three of 'em, dressed all in white. Elsie in a long white robe and a big white turban and carrying a big old white Bible and Jack and Jim wearing white suits and white ties and carrying big old white guitars. It took your breath away! Then Elsie would lay that Bible down and Jack and Jim would start playing them guitars and it would all begin. (*Hal has picked up the guitar. Sings.*)

> How do you do, ever'body, how do you do,
>> How do you do, ever'body, how do you do,
> This is Elsie, Jack, and Jim,
>> Come to save you from your sins,
> How do you do, ever'body, how do you do.

(*On the repeat Hal encourages the audience to respond, for it is becoming a tent meeting.*)

> How do you do, ever'body, how do you do,
>> How do you do, ever'body, how do you do,
> This is Elsie, Jack, and Jim,
>> Come to save you from your sins,
> How do you do, ever'body, how do you do.

> Ah-men!

And then Elsie would start to preach! And Jack and Jim would start taking up collection. And then there'd be more singing and more preaching and more collecting and more singing and more preaching and more collecting till there wouldn't be thirty cents left in that whole tent.

By this time Elsie would really be rolling. She'd snatch that turban off her head and about four or five foot of the reddest hair you ever seen would come flailing out. People would be rolling on the ground, talking in tongues, climbing the tent poles, howling like dogs, hopping and screaming and Elsie leading them on.

Then she'd call for the sick and up the aisle they'd come. Pushing and shoving and hobbling and crawling and on each one Elsie would lay her hands, roll her eyes, swing her head, and talk so loud and so fast you couldn't understand a word she said. But we knew. She was a-talking to God and waiting for His answer.

And sure enough, she'd finally lay her hands on some pore soul and you could tell it was happening. Ever' part of Elsie would freeze except her head and that would be swinging around like a gourd on a string. Then, with her hair all tangled up in Jack's guitar and the sweat a-pouring offa her, we'd hear the sound of God's answer. It would start low and just keep a-building. It seemed to come out of the air right around Elsie. It sounded like a cross between a buzz saw and a dehorned cow. It got so loud ever'body in that whole tent would shut up.

Then, with God's answer a-screeching and a-howling, that pore sick person would get up out of that bed or throw down them crutches and start to dance and sing and praise God. Well sir! Elsie on her knees a-crying and a-praying, Jack and Jim a-playing and a-singing; that whole tent just-a going wild . . ! You don't need no better heaven than that.

And then, "POP!" they'd be back behind that curtain and old Jesus a-smiling right on.

It was a funny thing. Nobody from Opp was ever healed. It was always some stranger from somewhere else that nobody knew. One night though, Tyrone Price's mama made him get in line with the sick because he'd been having so much trouble with his stomach. By this time old Tyrone weighed pretty close to five hundred pounds and I don't think there was ever anything wrong with his stomach; it just never got no rest. And old Tyrone didn't want to go and his mama was pushing and shoving and yelling at him and ever'body was laughing.

But by the time Tyrone got up on that stage he had the spirit. He was hopping and skipping and crowing like a rooster and when Elsie laid her hands on him he squalled like a stuck hog and jumped about four foot right straight up in the air. He just seemed to hang there a minute and when he come down that whole stage fell in. Boards was flying, old Jesus was falling, Elsie was scrambling, Jack and Jim was trying to save their guitars; it looked like a bomb had struck.

And when the dust settled, there was old Tyrone setting square on the head of the feller who'd been selling fans at the door. He'd been under that stage with a little victrola getting ready to make that sound we thought was God's answer.

Elsie, Jack, and Jim disappeared behind the curtain and that's the last we ever heard of them. 'Course most people was pretty put out, but not old Tyrone. He just set there on that pore feller's head all night a-playing that victrola over and over and ever' time the sound got real loud Tyrone'd bounce up and down and laugh his fool head off. And you know something? Tyrone never complained about his stomach again. Elsie, Jack, and Jim delivered!

Prayer meetings! Why did I remember that? Oh, I know. It's because I think we all have a kinda second religion; sorta like Shintoism where you worship your ancestors. You see, I think we all want something real from our past; a pocketknife, a lamp, a jar . . something we've touched and kept that makes us sure it all really happened.

PAPA

(*offstage*) I knowed it was all gonna go bad when you run off with this boy's paw . .

HAL

(*firmly*) No! Now, we've told them enough already!

KATE

No! Now I'm telling you, no!

HAL

(*firmer*) I'm telling *you* no! We've said enough! (*During the following Hal enters the kitchen, hooks the screen door, "blows" out the lamp, and places the chairs firmly under the table.*) I think we've made our point, we don't need this one. There are some things I'd rather not remember.

PAPA

(*offstage*) Looks like he's filling out already. (*Hal looks up into the flies suspiciously. Papa chuckles offstage.*) We ain't like the Glanceys, are we boy? (*Hal relaxes a little and laughs.*)

HAL

No, Papa, we ain't like the Glanceys.

KATE

(*offstage laughing*) Papa, hush! I declare, you're worse'n any old bum in Opp . .

HAL

Well, we could tell that. That one was kinda funny.

182

PAPA

(*offstage angry*) I knowed it was all gonna go bad when you run off with this boy's paw! (*The lights are beginning to dim against Hal's will.*)

HAL

Wait a minute! I didn't say I'd remember that!

KATE

(*offstage*) No! Now I'm telling you, no! (*Hal paces the stage trying to stop what is happening.*)

HAL

Stop it! I won't remember that. You have to do what *I* say! (*The stage-lights have changed leaving Hal in a spot with everything else in darkness except the screen door which is silhouetted. The figure of a man stands outside the door. There are several sharp raps that rattle the hook on the door.*)

PAPA

Kate? Kate! (*more raps*)

HAL

No, Papa!

PAPA

Kate? (*The door rattles.*)

HAL

Go away, Papa! We don't need this one!

PAPA

Kate, open this door!

HAL

(*screams*) NO!

PAPA

Kate? Kate? (*Papa continues knocking and calling ad lib. Against his will, Hal slowly pulls his shirttail out of his trousers and turns to face the door. His spot fades.*)

HAL

(*most unwillingly*) Who is it?

PAPA

Kate? Open the door! (*Hal is slowly, emotionally entering the scene.*)

HAL

Who is it?

PAPA

Harol', is that you? Open the door! Make haste! (*As Hal moves re-*

luctantly toward the door we hear two long low blasts from the cotton mill. Hal unhooks the door.)

HAL

Papa?

PAPA

That you, Harol'?

HAL

That you, Papa? (*Papa enters the dark kitchen.*)

PAPA

Where's Kate? Ain't she up yet?

HAL

Mama ain't home yet.

PAPA

What're you doing here with the lights off? It's black as a Poland-china's ass. Put on some light. (*Hal strikes a match and "lights" the lamp. Papa is eight years older than when we first saw him. Still vigorous and strong but becoming more deliberate and slow. He is dressed in a white shirt buttoned at the throat and sleeves and cheap "store" pants. On his head is a flat-brimmed tan Stetson. Both Hal and Papa blink in the sudden light.*) Was you still in bed? You like a little rabbit, ain't you? Get some clothes on and get Papa a cup of coffee, shug.

HAL

I can't make you no coffee, Papa, I can't light the stove.

PAPA

You can't? (*Papa looks at the coal-oil stove disapprovingly.*) How come? You just put a match to it, don't you? You forget how to build a fire since you'all moved away from us?

HAL

Nossir! I can light it but Mama takes a thing, she calls a valve? She takes it with her when she goes to work. Said she was scairt I'd blow myself up. I wouldn't do no such-a-thing! (*Papa has been circling the room, looking it over. It is obvious he has never been here before.*)

PAPA

Well, if that don't beat all! You and your mama moving away from us, you can't light the fire, sleeping till dinner time; what you standing there holding that shirt for? (*Papa reaches over and flips Hal's shirttail in front. Hal laughs embarrassedly and turns upstage clutching the shirttail to him.*)

HAL

Don't, Papa!

PAPA

(*in great good spirits*) Well, look-a-there! You look like old man Wadford! You know his is sixteen inches long? That looked like a little corn silk sprouting down there. You growing up on me. You gonna have to stop sitting on Papa's lap. How old are you, shug?

HAL

I was just twelve. Papa, I gotta pee! (*Hal quickly exits through the screen door. Dawn is breaking outside and we can see Hal's back as though urinating into the yard. Papa looks around at Kate's new home. He sees there is no solid door leading outside.*)

PAPA

You'all need a door on that. It don't seem chilly out there but they's a draught in here. Kate shore ain't moving up is she? All I can see I like is that stove and it don't work. This place ain't worth a penny a box! (*Hal re-enters tucking in his shirttail.*)

HAL

Papa, can I fix you a glass of sugar and water? (*Papa meets this hospitality with a great deal of respect.*)

PAPA

No, Harol', I et with your granny before I went yonder. You et?

HAL

Nossir. Mama'll fix something when she gets home.

PAPA

What time she get off?

HAL

At six. I heard the whistle when you was knocking.

PAPA

You did? I don't hardly never miss it but I did. Well, she oughta be home. (*Hal takes a pocket watch from his pocket.*)

HAL

It'll be a few more minutes. It's ten after now. (*Papa reacts slightly to the watch.*)

PAPA

You got a watch there?

HAL

Yessir. It was for my birthday. Mama let me buy it at Elmore's. It cost seventy-eight cents and seven tokens. It don't have "shine-in-the-dark," them was a dollar. But I like this one better. (*Papa relaxes and is very pleased for Hal.*)

PAPA

Your birthday? Let me see it. (*Papa takes the watch and holds it carefully near the lamp to see it.*) Well, sir! I ain't never seen one just like that. Look how clear them numbers is. Is it a Ingersol? (*Hal takes the watch.*)

HAL

It ain't no Ingersol but they said at Elmore's it was just as good.

PAPA

You take care of that and it'll last you a time.

HAL

I'm gonna plait me a fob soon as I get me some leather. (*A step is heard outside and Kate can be seen through the screen.*) Here she is. Hi, Mama! Papa's here! (*The door opens and Kate enters. She looks thirty years older than when we first saw her. Her face is drawn with tiredness and her shoulders droop. She has been on her feet for twelve hours at the cotton mill and has now walked a mile home. She moves as though the varicose veins in her legs will burst. Her hair and brows are full of cotton lint and there is lint on her clothes. She still wears her work apron and she carries a pair of cheap felt slippers which she wears always except when walking outside. Kate looks at Papa as she enters and it is apparent they have drifted far apart. At this moment he is neither welcome nor unwelcome.*)

KATE

(*to Hal*) You're up. I seen the light. I figured you'd left the lamp lit all night again. (*She turns toward the stove.*) Hey, Papa.

PAPA

(*very cordial*) Hey, sister, good morning to you. (*Kate puts a valve into place on the coal-oil tank and "lights" the stove with a match. She shakes the coffeepot to see if there is cold coffee and then places the pot over the burner.*)

KATE

You want a cup of coffee?

PAPA

Much obliged. I could stand a cup. (*Kate sits heavily and removes her shoes.*)

KATE

I don't know what's worse. Standing all night or walking home. (*She hands the shoes to Hal with a look of distaste.*) Put 'em on the porch, hon. They smell so bad. (*Hal takes the shoes and exits through the screen door. Kate calls after him.*) You eat?

HAL

No'm, I just got up. (*Hal re-enters, gets a stool, and sits near Papa's feet.*)

KATE

It don't matter, I reckon. You eat like a bird. You was the fattest baby. (*Kate rises and sets the table for coffee.*)

PAPA

Now, sister, he'll fill out when he's ready. (*Kate catches sight of herself in the mirror and tiredly begins pulling lint from her hair.*) From the looks of him when I woke him up, he's filling out already. (*Kate looks at the two of them for a moment, then sees Hal's embarrassment and realizes what Papa is talking about. She laughs in spite of herself.*)

KATE

Papa, hush. I declare, you're as bad as any old bum in Opp.

PAPA

(*mock seriousness*) Well, he was, Kate. I don't know about you two living off over here by yourself. We never had nothing like that in our family. (*Papa looks at Hal, laughs, and winks.*) We ain't like the Glanceys, are we, boy? (*Kate smiles and then laughs.*)

KATE

Humph! We had worse'n that in this family that I can remember. I'd hate to find out what happened before I was born.

PAPA

Now, Kate, the Bible says, "love one another."

KATE

Now, stop that. Your jokes are better off in the barn. Ernie said he saw you and half the riffraff in Opp standing around sniggering your heads off Saturday.

PAPA

(*elaborate unconcern*) Who did? Ernie? That the outlander you been seeing? Well, I never knowed his name. (*Kate is a little flustered at the mention of Ernie's name and primps unconsciously. She pours coffee for herself and Papa and serves Papa's with a saucer. Kate sits at the opposite side of the table as Papa saucers his coffee and sips. To Hal*) Hand me the salt, will you, shug. Your mama never makes it salty enough. (*Hal rises and hands Papa the salt box. Papa pours a small amount of salt into his palm, then puts the salt into the cup and the last few grains into the saucer. He stirs and tastes. It is fine.)*

KATE

Harol', I'm too tired to fix your breakfast. Are there any cornflakes? Have that, won't you, shug? (*Hal goes to the cupboard and gets cornflakes, bowl, spoon, and a jar of milk and brings them to the table. He prepares his breakfast during the following.)*

HAL

Papa, Ernie used to live on a farm that had a tractor! He said their farm was over five hundred acres!

PAPA

Five hundred acres? Pshaw! That right, Kate?

KATE

That's what he tells Harol'. If it's true it's a way yonder. Where was it, Harol'?

HAL

Oregon. That's a state. Papa, Ernie's been a sergeant in the United States Army fifteen years. Says he makes ever'body march. (*Hal smells the jar of milk and wrinkles his nose.*) Mama, this milk is sour.

KATE

It is? (*She smells the milk.*) I swear, I think Mrs. Breedlove's selling me old milk. Well, put some more sugar on it. This will have to do till Friday.

PAPA

You getting serious, Kate? That how come you moved out? (*Kate giggles in spite of herself. The romance with Ernie is very important.*)

KATE

No. Oh, I don't know. Harol' likes him pretty good, don't you? (*Hal doesn't answer but moves away to sit on the trunk and eat his cereal. Kate becomes serious.*) But you know why I moved out. Let's don't go back over that. You want something to eat?

PAPA

No, sister, I've et.

KATE

Then I think I'll lie down. I'm all right till I set and then I just get tired all over.

PAPA

In a minute. I want to talk to you and not about why you left. 'Course that's behind it but there ain't no grudge. Since you been gone we really been hit hard for money. Your ma's been poorly and Bessie don't make nearly the money you do. How come she can't get as good a job as you?

KATE

(*for the thousandth time*) At that cotton mill it's piece work, can't you understand? We got the same job. As hard as I can work I make nine dollars ever' two weeks. As hard as Bessie can work she makes five dollars. I can't help that!

PAPA

All right, don't get upsot. The thing is, I'm taking a job.

KATE

You? Why you don't know nothing but farming! (*Papa is trying to keep this conversation on as light a level as possible.*)

PAPA

Your daddy knows more'n you think. (*Papa winks at Hal.*) Don't he, shug? (*Hal nods enthusiastically.*) Porter More is gonna put me on as the town night watchman. They ain't never had nobody like that in Opp, but I asked if he knowed of anything and he said they was gonna have a watchman and he said I could have it. It works ever' night and pays fifty cents.

KATE

Thank God, you're finally doing something!

PAPA

Well, it ain't what I want, especially since I have to tote a gun. You know I never toted no gun 'less I needed to. I got your brother Edlo's pistol yesterday. (*Hal is very impressed. He puts his bowl on the cupboard and goes back to the stool at Papa's feet.*)

HAL

Papa, you gonna tote a gun? If I see you in town will you be toting a gun?

PAPA

Yeah, shug, from now on when you see me in town, I'll be toting that damn gun!

HAL

Boy howdy!

KATE

I'm proud you're working. You ain't made a dime farming since the year I come back with Harol'. You been on a different place ever' year and you ain't made a pair of overalls. And it means my leaving done some good, too.

PAPA

Now I said there wasn't no grudge but there ain't no use in talking that-away. We're farm people. We always been farm people. There ain't no good gonna come outta all this. You and Bessie working in that mill, now me, working in town. Toting a gun! I never toted a gun 'less I was after somebody, now I'm just-a toting after anybody! I knowed it was all gonna go bad when you run off with this boy's paw.

KATE

All right, say what you want but leave Mr. Ryan out of it. He never done nothing to you. I'm still proud you're working, but I'm gonna go to bed. I'm just too tired. (*It has gotten very light now. Kate "blows" out the lamp and moves to go off.*)

PAPA

Wait a minute, sister, I didn't come to what I come for. I got a gun but what I'm gonna have to have is a watch. (*Kate figures quickly.*)

KATE

Well . . I can let you have probably two dollars Friday. I'll tell Mr. Danley he'll just have to wait.

PAPA

Well, no, I don't want no two dollars.

HAL

I can't let you have my watch, Papa.

PAPA

That's all right, shug, I need a good watch. (*to Kate*) Kate, I need a real good watch.

KATE

I can't help you then. Two dollars is all I can do.

PAPA

What about that watch you brought back from Birmingham? I been thinking that watch is just what I need. Ain't that a railroad watch?

KATE

I'm sorry, I can't let you have that. That was Mr. Ryan's watch. That's all I got from him. That's gonna be Harol's.

PAPA

Now, I got to have that watch! I can't be walking the streets of Opp all night without no watch. You can't expect that of me.

KATE

There's a clock over the bank . .

PAPA

That's pore man's time! I been on pore man's time all my life but now I want that watch and I'm gonna have it!

KATE

No! Now, I'm telling you no! That's my husband's watch. That's all I got for four years of my life. That watch and this boy! You can't have the watch!

PAPA

Dammit to hell! Don't you tell me no! Where is it? (*Papa moves to the trunk but Kate jumps in front of him and for the first time in her life she lays her hands on her father in anger. She shoves Papa back but with one sweep of his arm he sends her crashing into the wall.*) God damn it! I come over here and I asked you for that watch and I want it and I'm gonna get it! I'll show you to stand in front of me! (*Papa rips open the trunk and begins throwing clothing about. Kate jumps at his back and Papa really hits her. She falls sobbing to the floor.*)

HAL

Papa, you're hurting her! (*Hal moves as though to help Kate as Papa lifts the tray from the trunk. He turns and hits Hal in the stomach with the tray and Hal and the tray crash down across the room.*)

KATE

God damn you! You never change! You take that watch and I'll kill you! (*Papa has found the watch. It is a beautiful watch with a gold knife and chain.*)

PAPA

You better shut your mouth before I fix you good. Ain't I your daddy? You want people to laugh because your own daddy ain't got no watch? You always been a hellcat, Kate, but I'll take it out of you!

KATE

You son of a bitch! (*Kate charges but Papa has a heavy piece of clothing in his hand and he beats her to the floor with it.*)

HAL

Don't hit her again! (*Hal grabs a butcher knife from the cupboard and advances uncertainly.*) That's my daddy's watch! You ain't got no right! (*Papa moves over, easily slaps the knife from Hal's hand, bends his arm behind him, wraps the piece of clothing around his head, and slams him to the floor in the corner.*)

PAPA

You little harrican-assed-shit! (*to the room in general*) By God, that's

191

what happens when you let families split up! That's why you moved out, ain't it? So the two of you could set yourselves up over your own daddy! Well, I'll beat the tar outta both of you! I know how to fix you! (*Papa starts to remove his thick leather belt but Kate grabs the butcher knife from the floor and quickly gets to her feet.*)

KATE

I'll cut you! Lay another hand on me or mine and by Jesus, I'll butcher you like a hog! (*Papa moves at her but there is nothing weak about her now and instead of retreating she advances. Papa stops, uncertain.*)

PAPA

Put that knife down before you get hurt! I'm telling you, Kate, put that knife down!

KATE

Don't tell me nothing! Just put that watch down and get out of my house and don't you never come back! Can't you understand? That watch and that boy is all I got from my husband!

PAPA

I understand! I understand when a daughter turns on her own flesh and blood! I understand when a daughter tries to cut her own daddy! I need this watch and I'm taking this watch! And you know what I think? I don't think you ever had a husband! All I know is you left, you was gone four years and you come back with this boy. You raising him like this watch! You're keeping him in that trunk! You don't want him to be no part of the family! All you do is tell him how to be different! Well, I'm keeping this watch!

KATE

Then, by God, keep the boy! You want ever'thing, then take ever'thing! Take it all, you worthless old whore-hopper! Take it all! I got somewhere to go and I'm going! (*As she talks she begins to pick up some clothing, still clutching the knife.*) You've spent your life taking what you want! Well, if you ever come at me again I'll tear you apart! And don't you worry about whether I had a husband! I ain't ashamed of nothing I ever done! (*Hal has been huddled in the corner and now he screams with a sound that goes all the way back to childhood.*)

HAL

MAMA!

KATE

Shut up, Harol'! You're as bad as the rest of them! All you want is to grow up just like 'em! Well, go on, I'm getting out! (*Kate's arms are full of clothes and Papa takes a step toward her but the knife comes up. He stops.*) If you have to find me I'll be with Ernie, but by God, if you don't want to get shot you better have a reason for finding me! (*As she moves past the stove she lays her hand on it for a moment. Then backing out the door she is gone. Papa stands uncertainly for a moment, puts a piece of clothing in the trunk, shifts uneasily. Hal has turned and sits looking at Papa. He makes no sound but Papa reacts as though he is crying very hard. Papa sits at the table.*)

PAPA

Now, hush, shug. We all just had a little fight. Your maw's like that. (*Papa takes the watch from his pocket and winds it.*) What time is it, shug?

HAL

Twenty-five minutes to seven. (*Papa sets the watch and listens to it with pleasure.*)

PAPA

Hush, now. (*Papa moves over to Hal, squats down but doesn't touch him.*) Hush, you hear? Now, I'll tell you what. I'm going to town. Wash your face and go on over to the house. We killed that little Duroc shoat yesterday. Your granny's rendering cracklings. Smell's mighty good. Go on over now, I'll see you at supper. (*Papa stands, puts the watch in his watch pocket, and drapes the chain into his pocket. It looks very nice. Finally he moves out the door, turning in the opposite direction from Kate. Hal gets up and looks out the door after Kate for a moment. He takes the watch from his pocket and looks at it and then moves down to the table and sits.*)

HAL

I shoulda let Papa have my watch. (*His eyes slowly wander around the chaos of the room. Finally he puts the watch gently on the table.*) I shoulda let him have my watch. (*The lights change to general lighting as before and Hal turns and faces the audience.*) Yesterday is gone and I can't be sure I was back there in yesterday because . . well, I never knew my daddy and my mother moved away while I was still a boy. I tried to catch up with her but then there was the service and then most ever'body was dead. And I never really got back to Opp and I never got anything to keep from any of them. So . . I wander a lot . . (*indicates the set*) . . and I build things that remind me of home. (*Hal takes the guitar and moves down front. The lights change leaving the sets in silhouette and Hal in a spot.*) I had to tell you all this so you would

193

understand this last. My mama used to always talk about how my daddy played the guitar. She said it was the prettiest thing, all covered with pearl. I remember I used to dream about my daddy's guitar although I'd never seen it. A few months ago I went to a furniture auction in Los Angeles looking for a couch and there in amongst the hall-trees and sideboards there was a little guitar case. And in the case was this little guitar. (*Hal runs his finger along the mother-of-pearl decoration.*) All covered with pearl. Seventy-five years old if it's a day. There was a tag on it that said, "Bekins Storage, Birmingham, Alabama." There was a number on the tag and I guess if I wanted to I could find out more about it. But, I don't think I will. I've waited too long for my daddy's guitar to find out it wasn't his. (*Hal strums a chord on the guitar.*) I've been told that my daddy liked this song so I guess I've got two things of his. (*sings*)

> Rattlesnake, oh, rattlesnake,
>> What makes your teeth so white?
> I been living in the bottom all of my life,
>> And I ain't done nothing but bite,
> Ain't done nothing but bite.

> Bluejay, oh, bluejay,
>> What makes you fly so high?
> Been a-robbing your corn field all of my life,
>> It's a wonder I don't die,
> It's a wonder I don't die.

(*The lights slowly fade to black.*)

THE END

SUPPLEMENTARY MATERIAL

The following is the radio program for Act One:

Old-time radio static. Jimmy Rodgers singing "T for Texas."

ANNOUNCER
You've been listening to the "Singing Brakeman," Jimmy Rogers, brought to you over WSM, Nashville, Tennessee, the Blue Network, by Purina Laying Mash. (*chimes*) And now, Black Draught, the time-honored laxative, brings you "Little Jimmy and His Dad."

DAD
Hello, Little Jimmy.

LITTLE JIMMY

(*he's a young boy*) Hello, Dad.

DAD

How are you today?

LITTLE JIMMY

Well, Dad, I was a little out of sorts this morning but Mama — uh — Mother give me a dose of Children's Black Draught and I feel real good now.

DAD

Good boy, Little Jimmy. Black Draught sure works. What's your first song?

LITTLE JIMMY

Well, Dad, I want to sing a song for Mother.

DAD

I know just the one you mean, Little Jimmy. (*Little Jimmy sings "Letter Edged in Black" with guitar accompaniment.*)

3 Miles to Poley by Hal Lynch was presented on November 5, 1971, at Theatre West in Los Angeles. It was directed by Joshua Bryant. Original music by Hal Lynch.

Cast of Characters

MAMA	Jan Burrell
PAPA	Wright King
HAL	Hal Lynch
HOBE	John Rayner